D1357374

Irish Peaks

Irish Peaks

Edited for the Federation of
Mountaineering Clubs
of Ireland by Joss Lynam

Constable London

First published in Great Britain 1982
by Constable and Company Limited
10 Orange Street, London WC2H 7EG
Copyright © 1982 by Federation of
Mountaineering Clubs of Ireland
ISBN 0 09 462570 0
Set in 9pt Times by
Inforum Ltd, Portsmouth
Printed in Great Britain by
Ebenezer Baylis & Son Ltd
The Trinity Press
Worcester and London

Contents

Illustrations

Preface

It is several years since Constable wrote to us suggesting a pictorial walking guide to the Irish hills on the lines of W. A. Poucher's *Scottish Peaks* and others. The Federation of Mountaineering Clubs of Ireland accepted the challenge and I, quite light-heartedly, agreed to edit it. I realized that I had neither Poucher's ability as a photographer, nor his leisure (and knowledge) to check out all the routes. However, I knew that, since it was an FMCI project, I could count on a great deal of help from my fellow Irish mountaineers. I have certainly had this help, but I seriously underestimated the time it would take to prepare the book and, especially to find the photographs we needed.

Since this book is a companion volume to Pouchers' I should mention the differences. We have not marked routes on the photographs, as we think the descriptions and maps suffice and that marked routes often create an illusion of a definite line, which on the untracked Irish hills would be misleading. I have omitted the section on equipment, which is handled very adequately in a number of other books, and on photography – through ignorance!

The walker who is used to the hills of Britain or Continental Europe will find two main differences in the Irish hills: there are far fewer people on the hills, and there are practically no paths. To my mind, both these factors add greatly to the enjoyment of the hills. I confess that coming, tired, off a Scottish or Cumbrian mountain in the mist I have been glad of cairns or footpaths, but how much greater is the sense of achievement in navigating one's way off a mountain with map, compass and watch.

Solitude is one of the delights of the Irish hills. The Wicklow Hills and the Mournes, close to Dublin and Belfast respectively, are relatively crowded at weekends, but elsewhere you will hardly meet more than one or two other parties, even on the more popular hills. This means that there has been relatively little problem with access (except, again, in the Mournes and Wicklow) since few farmers object to the occasional walker crossing their land. This does, however, require a responsible and careful attitude from all who walk on the Irish hills, so that this happy state may continue. Please remember that others will come after you; ask permission (even if it seems unnecessary), close gates, avoid crops (not forgetting that many pastures are cut for hay), do not damage walls or fences, remove your litter, and disturb domestic animals as little as possible (in particular, if you have a dog keep it under control). You will find that country people not only permit you to cross their land, but they will often be glad of a few words of chat. It would be rude and foolish not to respond.

Undoubtedly the lack of people and paths necessitates a little more caution on the part of the walker; you cannot expect to get directions from other walkers on your route, and map and compass are absolutely essential.

Clothing and equipment are basically the same as for comparable hills elsewhere. Irish hills are probably wetter underfoot than most, and the walker should give thought to choosing footwear. It is, fortunately, no longer mandatory to condemn all footwear except leather boots, so I can confess to having used all sorts on the hills, mostly on the assumption that my feet were going to get wet anyhow and that I would prefer lightness and comfort to an illusory hope of staying dry. Wellies, or the latest compromise, bog-trotters, should also be considered. It should be remembered, however, that none of these variations is as safe as boots, especially when descending steep, wet, grassy slopes, and, unless you are an experienced walker, the classic advice to stick to boots still holds good.

We hope the information we have provided will help you to plan your walks and enjoy them – and, perhaps, to walk over the many pleasant Irish hills we have no space to describe, and thus to share in the delight which all the contributors have received over the years from the Irish hills.

But no guidebook is a substitute for map, compass, and commonsense, and ultimately only you yourself can be responsible for your safety and enjoyment in the hills.

Joss Lynam
Dublin
1982

Acknowledgements

The compilation of this guide has been very much a group project, and on my own behalf and that of the FMCI I should like to thank all who helped to write it: David Herman, Jean Boydell, Michael Casey, Eithne Kennedy, Liam Convery (east); Frank Martindale (south-east); Sean O Suilleabhain (south-west); Tony Whilde (west, flora and fauna); Gerry Foley, Patrick Simms (north-west, north); Dick Rogers (Mournes); Bairbre Sheridan (place names) and Ruth Lynam (geology). Whatever my own qualifications for editing this guide, there will be few who would question the qualifications of my collaborators!

I am grateful also to the many photographers who helped and whose contributions are acknowledged in the list of illustrations. One notable contributor was Mr W. A. Poucher himself, whose quite brief visit, described in *Journey into Ireland*, produced many excellent photographs, some of which we have been glad to use. It is a pleasure to record the helpful co-operation of Bord Fáilte Eireann and the Northern Ireland Tourist Board in providing photographs.

I have also to thank Clodagh Lynam who drew the maps, and all the typists who made sense out of the contributors' handwriting, especially Jean Boydell who coped with contrasting varieties of Lynam family orthography.

I must thank my collaborators of Constable, publishers; Miles Huddleston for his patience in waiting as each deadline approached, and his faith, as each deadline passed manuscriptless, that the guide would eventually materialize; and Prudence Fay who patiently rationalized and corrected our carefree spellings of place names.

Lastly, my thanks are due to my wife, Nora, without whose help, patience, and forbearance, neither this book nor many other projects could have been completed.

J. L.
1982

KEY MAP

Scale of Miles

10 0 10 20 30

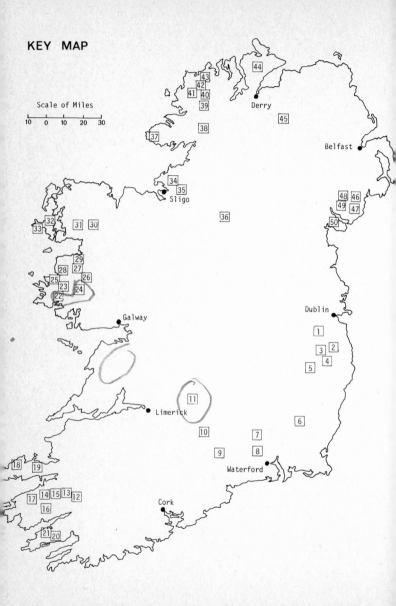

Introduction

Geology

According to modern geological theory, the earth's crust is made up of many plates which drift independently. When plates collide, one of the results is crumpling and disturbance of the plate margins, in which there is general uplift of the zone, and some material is buried and subjected to heat and pressure. These effects may be so extreme that the buried material melts and rises towards the surface again, forming great blisters of liquid which solidify slowly, becoming coarse-grained, crystalline rocks, such as granite or gabbro. If the blisters break through to the surface, the molten material pours out and quickly cools, to form fine-grained volcanic rocks – basalt for example. The final result of such a collision is a new mountain range.

In time the new range is worn down to a series of rounded stumps, such as we see in the mountains of Ireland, exposing the underlying granites and metamorphic rocks. However, the Irish mountain landscape has been rejuvenated by glaciation, which produced sharp peaks and steep-sided valleys from what would have been a gentle plateau landscape. Remnants of such a plateau can be seen in the flat summits of Devil's Mother and Mweelrea in Connemara, the Comeraghs in Waterford, and some parts of the Wicklow Mountains.

Irish mountain geology is dominated by two main mountain-building episodes, known as the Caledonian and Hercynian. The NE–SW oriented Caledonian episode took place over a long period, ending about 450 million years ago. Sandstones, shales and limestones were metamorphosed to become quartzites, gneisses, schists, and marbles, now found in Connemara, Mayo, Donegal, and Tyrone; later granites were introduced in these areas, and also in East Leinster and near Newry (Knocklayd). Quartzite is an extremely resistant rock and, though it often occurs in thin bands it still tends to form prominent peaks, which are characteristically steep and cone-shaped. There are many examples – Errigal,

Muckish, Slieve League, Slieve Snaght (on Inishowen) in Donegal; the Twelve Bens (Benbaun) and the Maumturks in Connemara; Nephin, Corranabinnia, Croaghaun in Mayo. Granite is also a very hard rock but it is susceptible to chemical attack, and as successive layers are peeled away, rounded, often dome-shaped mountains are formed. Slieve Snaght (Derryveagh) in Donegal, the Wicklow Range, Mount Leinster and Knocklayd are made up of granite intruded at the end of the Caledonian episode. Mount Leinster, Mullaghcleevaun, Tonelagee, Kippure, Lugnaquillia are all characteristic granite mountains, although their flanks have been modified and steepened by glacial action. Lugnaquillia is mainly granite, but the summit rock is the shaly remnant of the original roof over the granite blister. The relatively low rolling Croaghgorms in Donegal are also granite mountains.

While the Caledonian upheaval was still going on, Connemara and South Mayo were covered by the sea, and huge thicknesses of sandstones, conglomerates, and shales were laid down. Much of this was folded in the final stages of the Caledonian. Then a general uplift of the area produced a high plateau, which was gradually dissected by rivers and whose relief was much later exaggerated by glaciation. Mweelrea, Devil's Mother, Ben Gorm all have broad flat summits and are separated by deep glacial valleys which often follow weaknesses such as fractures or, as in the case of Glenummera, a soft shale band. Croagh Patrick, made of sediments of the same age, marks the site of an ancient submarine channel where highly quartz-rich sandstones (sedimentary quartzites) were deposited, and shows the characteristic cone-shaped quartzite outline.

Around the same time as the Leinster granite was emplaced, about 400 million years ago when the Caledonian disturbance had finally ended, Ireland became part of a large European landmass with a desert climate, and vast amounts of the reddish-coloured sandstones and shales known as Old Red Sandstone accumulated. Then the sea encroached again, and in the warm shallow waters limestones were laid down on top of the Old Red Sandstone and were followed by a variety of sandstones, shales, and limestones (including coal measures). Limestone can be dissolved by rainwater, and, where it is exposed, as in the Burren in Co. Clare, a karst landscape is produced, with caves, ephemeral lakes, limestone pavements, and very little surface drainage.

However, about 340 to 280 million years ago a second mountain-building episode, known as the Hercynian, took place. The main zone of deformation lay to the south of Ireland along an approximately E–W line, but the Old Red Sandstone and limestone of Cork and Kerry were compressed and folded. When the folds were subjected to weathering, the limestone was removed from the up-folds (anticlines) exposing the hard sandstone cores which resisted further erosion. The result was a series of parallel high sandstone ridges, such as the peninsulas of Iveragh and Beara, including many prominent peaks – Mullaghanattin, Knocknagantee, Coomacarrea, Carrauntoohil and the Reeks, Purple Mountain, Mangerton on the Iveragh Peninsula; Hungry Hill and Eskatarriff on the Beara Peninsula; Brandon and Baurtregaum on the Dingle Peninsula. To the north, further from the main Hercynian zone, the folds are broader and gentler, but have weathered out in a similar way. The Comeraghs, the Galtees, Knockmealdowns, and Keeper Hill are all isolated inliers of upfolded Old Red Sandstone (and older rocks) surrounded by low-lying limestone country.

The last major disturbance to affect Ireland was extensive rifting and associated volcanic activity centred along the Irish Sea about 70 to 50 million years ago. At this time the Mourne Mountains granite was emplaced. These mountains, though generally steeper than those of the Leinster granite, show the same rounded or dome-shaped outlines.

The most recent geological event to have a major effect on Irish mountain landscape was the glaciation of the Ice Ages. Though a relatively minor event, its impact on the landscape was great as there have been no modifying influences since. The Ice Ages were periods of general cold during which the island was practically buried under ice. The first lasted from approximately 175,000 to 100,000 years ago, and the second from about 70,000 to 10,000 years ago. During each of these periods the ice receded and advanced several times and the cover was never complete – there was a separate small ice-cap over Cork and Kerry.

In mountain areas the ice had a mainly erosive effect. As the climate deteriorated small patches or lenses of ice built up in hollows, particularly on north- and east-facing slopes sheltered from sun and prevailing winds, and as a lens grew the weight of the ice forced it to creep downhill, becoming a glacier. The small high ice patches carved deep, steep-sided corries out of the hillsides, and the corrie glaciers amalgamated to form a valley glacier which exploited any existing valley or weakness, deepening and straightening it to produce a characteristic trough or U-shaped valley, with steep sides and a broad flat floor. Corries and U-shaped valleys are often now occupied by a lake or a string of lakes (paternoster lakes), or sometimes by an obviously inadequate stream which meanders across the valley floor. There are numerous examples of corries in Ireland – Coomshingaun in the Comeraghs is a well-known one, and others include the Lough Bray corrie below Kippure, Devil's Punch Bowl on Mangerton, and Coum Gowlaun north of Devil's Mother. The Doo Lough valley east of Mweelrea is a typical U-shaped glacial valley, as are the Poisoned Glen facing Errigal, Silent Valley in the Mournes, the Gap of Dunloe between Purple Mountain and the Reeks, and Glendalough in Wicklow where the stream still flows through its old valley before dropping steeply into the glacial trough.

In many cases, such as the Wicklow Mountains, the mountain tops would have protruded through the ice as nunataks, and would have been subjected to severe attack by frost. Constant freezing and thawing led to soils becoming so saturated with water that they would creep ('solifluct') downhill, exposing the underlying rock. If this was granite, the surface layers, weakened by chemical action, quickly disintegrated and soliflucted off the sounder layers, leaving a tower-shaped remnant known as a tor. Tors are conspicuous on summits and breaks of slope in the Mournes, and also occur in the Dublin and Wicklow Mountains. Water collecting in cracks expanded and contracted as it froze and thawed, and caused shattering of more resistant rocks, such as quartzite, producing huge amounts of the large angular fragments which make up scree.

When corries were excavated along opposite sides of a narrow ridge, a sharp steep-sided spine or arête was left, jagged and rotten from exposure to frost. Arêtes wind their way between the corries linking pyramidal-shaped peaks. The ridge connecting Carrauntoohil to Caher and Beenkeragh (the Lough Acoose Horseshoe) is a fine arête, circling the Coomloughra/Lough Eagher corrie.

Spillways are another type of spectacular valley associated with glaciation. When the ice began to melt, the meltwater was sometimes impounded between unmelted ice and surrounding hills, until it poured out through a gap in the hills scouring a deep gorge-like spillway.

Glacial deposits are a smaller-scale feature of mountainous areas. Moving ice carries large amounts of material on the surface of, below, and within, the ice. Debris carried on top of the glacier was sloughed off along the valley sides as lateral moraine, and when the ice melted the terrace thus formed indicates the depth of ice that once filled the valley. Other debris was dumped at the front of the glacier as terminal moraine. Where the front was stationary for a time a ridge of moraine built up across the valley, and series of these ridges marks the retreat of the ice. Terminal moraines often form dams containing present-day lakes. Material scraping over rocks at the base of the glacier left scratches which indicate the direction of flow.

Material transported by ice has also helped to determine the larger-scale pattern of ice movement – boulders originating in Connemara have been found in Kerry, for example. It is now known that during both glaciations the ice advanced initially from Scotland, proceeded down the Irish Sea, then spread out over Ireland, avoiding such barriers as the Wicklow Mountains. Later local ice centres developed in Ireland. The ice finally receded about 10,000 years ago, but the climate has continued to fluctuate. The modern boggy and peat-covered mountains are just a temporary phase while the climate remains wet and relatively temperate.

The weather
The two main factors which shape the weather in Ireland are the Atlantic Ocean and the westerly airflow of the middle latitudes. The westerly airflow brings us a succession of frontal systems, and the

ocean ensures that we do not get too cold in winter, or too warm in summer.

The depressions which cross the Atlantic mostly pass north of Ireland, and their associated fronts sweep across the country at a rate of 170 a year, each front bringing its quota of rain. It is no good pretending that Ireland does not get a lot of rain; it does, but because the fronts are generally fairly fast-moving, the rain rarely lasts for very long.

There is a definite seasonal pattern. The early winter (December and January) is characterized by rapidly moving depressions which bring strong winds – often gales – from the west, and heavy rainfall. In late winter and spring (February – May/June) the Continental high-pressure area tends to spread to Ireland and there are occasional visitations from the Greenland high. This produces drier weather, and May is generally the best month in the year. In late June and July the oceanic winds usually re-establish themselves, bringing more rain; and in August the combination of heat and high humidity often produces thunderstorms. In late August and September, cold northerly air masses cause depressions, but often there will be a week or two of fine anticyclonic weather. October and November are characterized by westerlies bringing frontal rain; in November the occasional anticyclone may again produce fine (but often foggy) weather.

Rainfall is perhaps the aspect of the weather that most affects the walker; March, April and May have the most dry days and December and January have the fewest. There is, of course, considerably more rain in the west, where the hills along the west coast force the clouds to rise and discharge their moisture. Most of the western hills have rain on more than 225 days in the average year, while the Mournes, Wicklow Hills and the sandstone mountains of the south-east have less than 200 days with rain. Even in the west there is a substantial difference as you move inland – to take an example in Connemara, when the rain is beating down on the Twelve Bens the hills around Lough Nafooey may be dry.

Apart from wetting the mountains when it falls, the rain has the further disadvantage that it causes the Irish hills to be mostly wet underfoot. Many of the valleys are boggy, and while the ridges are usually dry, there are also big wet plateaux (such as Maum Trasna) covered in bogland. This is not to say that there are not plenty of good hill walks (quite apart from the fifty mentioned in this book) which are mainly on dry ground, but it is true that, except in a dry summer, it is hard to walk the Irish hills (especially in the west) without a little bit of bog-trotting.

A second important aspect of the weather for the hill-walker is the prevalence of mist and cloud. The clouds will often descend to below 1,500 ft in the hills and this poses navigational problems – easily solved by the walker who has a map and compass and knows how to use them, but potentially dangerous for those who are unprepared.

Ireland gets very little snow. The Gulf Stream warms the west coast and so the Macgillycuddy's Reeks, which as the highest mountains in Ireland would be likely to have the greatest snowfall, rarely hold snow for very long. It is the Wicklow Hills, in the colder east, which generally hold the snow; almost every year Lugnaquillia will, for a few weeks, be a serious proposition even by the easiest route up Camara Hill. The Mournes also hold snow. In February, March, and April, though, the walker will often have a fine day on the hills with a dusting of snow brought by cold east or north-east winds, not sufficient to provide technical problems, but enough to brighten the sombre colour of the winter or early spring landscape.

The statistics of mist and rain are a little depressing, and perhaps suggest a picture of grey, drab walks in poor visibility. While this may well happen sometimes, a truer picture of Irish hill weather is changeability. There will rarely be a day on the hills when the wind will not blow the mist away and the sun gleam through the clouds to reflect off the streams and pick out the bright greens and russets of the hillsides. Especially in the early summer, there are plenty of days with blue skies and hardly a cloud.

The art of dealing with the weather in the Irish hills is the same as everywhere else – be prepared. Remember always that the temperature drops by anything up to 3°C per 1,000 ft of climb, and so a pleasant day at sea-level may be cold on the top of Lugnaquillia. Remember, also, that the wind is often $2\frac{1}{2}$ times as strong at 3,000 ft as it is at sea-level, so carry wind-proof clothing and a spare pullover, even if the sky is blue. For that matter, be prepared for rain even if the sky is blue!

For information about the weather, there are the usual forecasts on radio and television and in the newspapers. As in other countries, these are geared to sea-level activities and need intelligent interpretation for the hills. There are no special weather forecasts for mountaineers, but the Meteorological Office in Dublin is very ready to answer telephone queries and will generally be able to give you a fairly accurate local forecast. The relevant telephone numbers at present are 01–425555 (Dublin) and 061–62677 (Shannon). (There is also a 'dial-a-forecast' service in Dublin, but it is not of much use to the hill-walker.)

Flora and fauna

Ireland's mountains are low and small in extent compared with many ranges in Britain and on the Continent. And, in common with offshore islands elsewhere, the number of species of plants and animals which can be found here is smaller than on mainland Europe. But this is not to say that Ireland's mountains are uninteresting places for the naturalist. In fact, the attraction of Ireland's mountain flora was well summed up by Nathaniel Colgan in a paragraph from his often quoted article 'Botanical Notes on the Galway and Mayo Highlands' (*Irish Naturalist*, 1900).

It may sound like a paradox to say that botanical survey of an Irish mountain region derives a particular zest from the poverty of our flora in alpine species. Yet the assertion may be made with perfect truthfulness. That the rapture of discovery varies with the rarity of the object sought for, that the value of the thing attained is measured by the labour of attainment – these are time-honoured truisms in every system of proverbial philosophy; and their essential truth is daily borne in upon the mind of the botanist who devotes himself to the exploration of any of the mountain-groups of Ireland. The fans of the alpine club-moss, which he spurns with callous feet on the slopes of Snowdon, he half worships when they meet his longing eyes in the Wicklow or Kerry Highlands; and so with many others of our alpine species –

unconsidered trifles abroad, they become objects of enthusiasm at home.

The same sentiments apply to the mountain fauna, which is simple by European standards; but the sight of a fox with her cubs, a dipper bobbing on a mountain stream, or the shrill cry of the peregrine can bring infinite pleasure and excitement to a day in the hills.

But we are also lucky in Ireland, because our strongly maritime climate provides favourable conditions at low altitudes for many plants which, elsewhere, can be found only at considerable elevations or at high latitudes. The diminutive least willow (*Salix herbacea*), an Ice Age relic forced to retreat by an improving climate, still occurs on the high rocky ridges of most of our mountain ranges. But in the west, it can be found occasionally at elevations of less than 1,000 ft. Another interesting mountain plant, this time with its origins in the Pyrenees, is St Patrick's cabbage (*Saxifraga spathularis*), a native of Ireland, but absent from Britain. It occurs from sea-level to the top of Carrauntoohil, in its Kerry headquarters and on the high ridges of the Connemara and Donegal mountains, where it adds welcome colour to the bleak quartzites. It also occurs on the Galty Mountains (generally known as the Galtees) the Knockmealdowns and the Comeraghs and at two isolated sites in the Wicklow Hills.

Looking briefly at each range in turn, we find that the Mourne Mountains, with their impressive granite peaks, are, perhaps, the least interesting for the botanist. Generally speaking they support few alpine plants and not many other plants worthy of special note. On the high ground the following species have been recorded: starry saxifrage (*Saxifraga stellaris*); roseroot (*Sedum rosea*); alpine saw-wort (*Saussurea alpina*); water lobelia (*Lobelia dortmanna*) a species more common in the west; cowberry (*Vaccinium vitis-idaea*); least willow (*Salix herbacea*); a prostrate form of juniper (*Juniperus communis nana* = *J. sibirica*) generally restricted to the north and west; parsley fern (*Cryptogramma crispa*) a rare plant of the north and east; alpine club-moss (*Lycopodium alpinum*); and the quillwort (*Isoetes lacustris*) which typically fringes mountain loughs in the north and west. The Welsh poppy

(*Meconopsis cambrica*) occurs on the lower ground and the rare rose-bay willow herb (*Epilobium angustifolium*) grows on the high cliffs of Slieve Binnian and Eagle Mountain.

The Dublin and Wicklow mountains present the largest expanse of high ground in Ireland, some 200 square miles being above 1,000 ft; but, as with the Mournes, the heather-clad granite domes offer little of excitement to the botanist. Farmland predominates to about 900 ft where it gives way to heather moor (*Calluna vulgaris*) on the gentle slopes as they rise to the summits, which are carpeted with deer-grass (*Scirpus caespitosus*), cotton grass (*Eriophorum angustifolium*), woolly hairmoss (*Rhacomitrium lanuginosum*) and bog-mosses (*Sphagnum*). On the highest peak in the east of Ireland, Lugnaquillia, there have been recorded, in addition to the species already mentioned, such plants as bilberry (*Vaccinium myrtillus*), heath bedstraw (*Galium saxatile*), common mouse-ear chickweed (*Cerastium fontanum*) and alpine club-moss (*Lycopodium alpinum*) as well as several more common grasses, sedges, rushes, and mosses.

The Galtees are the most inland range in the country and therefore the most remote from maritime influences, and their flora generally reflects their location. Even the highest peak, Galtymore, has only a small flora, almost devoid of alpine plants. According to Praeger in *The Botanist in Ireland* the 'best plant of the Galtees is *Arabis (Cardaminopsis) petrara*', the northern rock-cress, which has only been recorded at two other sites in the British Isles, one in Leitrim, the other in the Cuillins of Skye. The cliff flora of the Galtees, the Knockmealdowns, and the Comeraghs, unaffected as it is by man or his grazing animals, will prove more interesting to the botanist than that of the hillsides. Lesser meadow-rue (*Thalictrum minus*), more common near the coast, has been recorded in the Galtees, as has mountain scurvy-grass (*Cochleria alpina*), rose-root, starry saxifrage, St Patrick's cabbage, cowberry, mountain sorrel (*Oxyria digyna*) least willow. Green spleenwort (*Asplenium viride*), another rarity which is mainly restricted to the western mountain, finds refuge on the cliffs of the Galtees and around the great coums of the Comeraghs.

Moving west to the Cork and Kerry mountains we enter a harsher environment, but one which will offer more interesting rewards in return for modest exertion. Carrauntoohil, the highest peak in the land, supports a varied alpine flora and even on its exposed summit about twenty species have been recorded. In addition to some of the species already mentioned (such as the saxifrages, bedstraw, bilberry, and heather) one can find tormentil (*Potentilla erecta*); thrift (*Armeria maritima*) a plant more familier on the coast; wild thyme (*Thymus drucei*); sorrel (*Rumex acetosa*); sheep's sorrel (*Rumex acetosella*); rushes (*Juncus*); greater wood-rush (*Luzula sylvatica*); fir club-moss (*Lycopodium selago*); and several species of grasses.

To the north-west, Mount Brandon offers some of the richest alpine grounds in the country in and around its large eastern coum. Here alpine lady's mantle (*Alchemilla alpina*) may be found at one of only three reported sites in the country. Alpine meadowgrass (*Poa alpina*) is another rarity which graces this fine mountain.

The lower, more barren, summits of the Connemara mountains are devoid of all but the toughest plants such as St Patrick's cabbage, the lichen *Cladonia* and some primitive club-mosses. In the Twelve Bens it is only on Muckanaght, where the more fertile schists rise to the summit, that a continuous carpet of vegetation can be found above 2,000 ft. Here, there are several rare alpine plants such as alpine meadow-rue (*Thalictrum alpinum*), purple saxifrage (*Saxifraga oppositifolia*), mountain sorrel, saw-wort, least willow and holly fern (*Polystichum longchitis*). The mountains of Mayo are less harsh than the Bens or the Maumturks and support a summit flora somewhat similar to that of Carrauntoohill.

The limestone hills of Sligo provide a sharp contrast in both form and flora. The flat-topped, cliff-girt plateau of Benbulbin and its associated peaks offer a wealth of material for the botanist. The plateau is covered with thick peat and the flora is typical of such an acid soil. But where the limestone projects, as on Truskmore, a variety of interesting species appear including tormentil, heath bedstraw, golden rod (*Solidago virgaurea*), bilberry, heather, common cow-wheat (*Melampyrum pratense*), crowberry (*Empetrum nigrum*) and the orchid *Dactylorhiza maculata*. However, the cliffs offer the most interesting, if most inaccessible, species in the forms of sandwort (*Arenaria ciliata*), alpine saxifrage

(*Saxifraga nivalis*) and chickweed willow-herb (*Epilobium alsinifolium*). The former is a particularly rare plant, occurring nowhere else in the British Isles, and the others occupy their only Irish station. Several other arctic/alpine and Lusitanian species are to be found on Benbulbin, as well as such relatively uncommon plants as the strawberry tree (*Arbutus unedo*) better known in the south; blue-eyed grass (*Sisyrinchium bermudiana*); and pink butterwort (*Pinguicula lusitanica*).

Across Donegal Bay, the landward slopes of Slieve League are an important resort for many of the alpine plants already mentioned. Surprisingly, the distinctive mountain avens (*Dryas octopetala*), familiar to Burren visitors, have been recorded here, many miles from their best known and major haunt. There are also some interesting non-alpine plants on the rich swards of Slieve League, including several uncommon hawkweeds (*Hieracium*).

Donegal is dominated by mountains linked by extensive bogs. It is washed on three sides by the Atlantic and its continuous exposure to harsh, wet winds has enabled (or forced) many alpine plants to descend to lower altitudes than elsewhere in the country. For example, hoary whitlow grass (*Draba incana*) occurs only from sea-level to a few hundred feet here, whereas it can be found at over 2,500 ft to the south. Purple saxifrage occurs from sea-level to nearly 2,000 ft, and summit species such as alpine meadow-rue and alpine saw-wort can be found below the 1,000-ft contour.

However, the warming influence of the Atlantic has also left its mark by allowing plants such as the Killarney fern (*Trichomanes speciosum*) and the maidenhair fern (*Adiantum capillus-veneris*) to thrive outside their more usual south-western haunts.

The animals of the Irish mountains are generally few in number, small in size, and secretive in their habits, so the walker must be ever watchful and, above all, patient if he wishes to study our native fauna. Birds will be the walker's most obvious companions and the ubiquitous meadow pipit (*Anthus pratensis*) will never be far away, flitting from rock to rock uttering its piping call. The skylark (*Alauda arvensis*) will fill the spring air with its familiar song as it hovers overhead. But, to me, the return of the 'chack-chack-chacking' whatever (*Oenanthe oenanthe*) in March or early April heralds the approach of spring and, hopefully, good weather in the mountains. The shrill call of the common sandpiper (*Tringa hypoleucos*) will greet the walker as he approaches many a mountain lough between April and June. The attractive dipper (*Cinclus cinclus*), a bird of the fast-flowing streams, dives to collect its animal food from the streambeds. But the monarch of the hills is the dark and husky raven (*Corvus corax*) flying easily along the glens and over the ridges of all our mountain ranges. Its smaller relation the chough (*Pyrrhocorax pyrrhocorax*) with its bright red legs and bill, is more restricted in its range, but can be seen in the mountains of Cork, Kerry and Connemara. The red grouse (*Lagopus lagopus*) is at home on the heather slopes of the Wicklow Mountains, but is less common in the west where the climate and heather are generally poorer. Winter visitors, such as the woodcock (*Scolopax rusticola*) and snipe (*Gallinago gallinago*) may startle the walker when they rise suddenly from under his feet, but skeins of white-fronted geese (*Anser albifrons*), flying silently to and from their secure mountain lough roosts, will restore a feeling of peace and tranquillity. The kestrel (*Falco tinnunculus*), hovering in search of food, is a common sight in the hills and the smaller merlin (*Falco columbarius*) is often seen in the western mountains. But of the birds of prey pride of place must go to the peregrine (*Falco peregrinus*), screaming fearsomely as it soars high over precipitous cliffs in remote glens.

Red deer (*Cervus elaphus*) once roamed freely through most of Ireland's mountains, but today, alas, wild herds occur only at Glenveagh in Donegal and in the Kerry and Wicklow Mountains. In the latter two ranges the introduced sika deer (*Cervus nippon*) is also common. But the commonest large mammals in the mountains are the fox (*Vulpes vulpes*) and the badger (*Meles meles*). Neither is seen frequently, but their regular paths are easily recognized. The Irish hare (*Lepus timidus*) is often seen in silhouette as it lopes over the horizon to safety. But the rabbit (*Oryctolagus cuniculus*), which is abundant on some fertile hillsides, is not as easy-going and scampers quickly to its burrow when disturbed. The red squirrel (*Sciurus vulgaris*) is a woodland species which is rare in the west but quite common on the wooded lower slopes of the mountains to the

east. One of our smaller animals, the long-tailed field mouse
(*Apodernus sylvaticus*) is probably Ireland's commonest mammal,
according to Dr James Fairley, who has even found it at the top of
Carrauntoohil!

One of the most interesting fish in Ireland is the char (*Salvelinus
alpinus*), an Arctic relic which inhabits some of the deep, cold
loughs in and around the western mountains. Then come the
'mountainy' brown trout (*Salmo trutta*) which can provide fine sport
in spite of their small size.

The invertebrate animals of the mountains have been little
studied and offer a fertile field of investigation for the hill-walking
naturalist. Butterflies can be seen occasionally at considerable
heights in the mountains, but only one species could be said to be a
truly mountain species. This is the elusive mountain ringlet (*Erebia
epiphron*), a butterfly of arctic/alpine origin which has only been
recorded on a few occasions in the west. A variety of other insects –
biting and non-biting – make themselves evident on the hills,
particularly during the summer months. Finally, an animal of some
renown is the Kerry spotted slug (*Geomalacus maculosus*) which I
have had the fortune to see on the Reeks. It is widely distributed
throughout Kerry and west Cork, but is found nowhere else in the
British Isles.

List of common Irish words describing mountain features

The names ascribed on the maps to features of the Irish hills are
mostly the best efforts of English-speaking surveyors to understand
and transliterate local Irish names given to them orally. It is no
wonder, therefore, that they have become a little mangled with the
passage of time. The commonest Irish words used for features, their
anglicized equivalents, and their English meanings, are listed below.

The words are given in the nominative case. It should be realized
that in the Irish language, when nouns are used in a qualifying
sense, the spelling in the genitive may change. Examples:

Bár Trí gCúm – 'Baurtregaum' – the top of the three coums (*Cúm* –
'coum' – nominative; *gCúm* – 'gaum' – genitive).
Ath na mBó – 'Annamoe' – the ford of the cows (*Bó* – 'bo' – cows –
nominative, *mBó* – 'moe' – genitive).

Abha, abhain (ow, owen) river
Achadh (agha, augh) field
Aill or *faill* cliff
Alt height or side of glen
Ard height, promontory
Ath (ath, ann) ford
Baile (bally) town, townland
Bán (bawn, baun) white
Barr top
Beag (beg) small
Bealach (ballagh) pass
Beann (ben) peak or pointed mountain
Bearna (barna) gap
Beith (beigh) birch tree
Bignian little peak
Boireann (burren) stony, rocky district
Bóthar (boher) road
Bóthairín (boreen) small (unsurfaced) road
Breac (brack) speckled
Brí (bree, bray) hill
Buaile (booley) summer dairy pasture
Bun foot of anything, river mouth
Buí yellow
Carn pile of stones
Carraig (carrick) a rock
Cathair (Caher) stone fort
Ceann (Ken) head, headland
Ceathramhadh (carrow) quarter of land
Ceapach plot of tillage ground
Cill cell, church
Clár plain, board
Cloch stone

Clochóg steppling stones
Cluain (cloon, clon) meadow
Cnoc (knock, crock) hill
Coill (kyle, kill) wood
Coire cauldron, corrie
Cor rounded hill
Corrán (carraun) sickle, serrated mountain
Cruach, cruachán steep hill (rick)
Cúm (coum) hollow, corrie, coum
Dearg red
Doire (derry) oakgrove
Druim ridge
Dubh (duff, doo) black
Dun fort, castle
Eas (ass) waterfall
Eisc (esk) steep, rocky gully
Fionn (fin) white, clear
Fraoch (freagh) heath, heather
Gaoith (gwee) wind
Glas green
Glais streamlet
Gleann (glen) valley
Gorm blue
Gort tilled field
Inbhear (inver) river mouth
Inis island
Lágh (law) hill
Leac flagstone
Leaca, leacán (lacken) side of a hill
Leacht huge heap of stones
Learg side of a hill
Leitir (letter) wet hillside
Liath (lea, leagh) grey
Loch (lough) lake or sea inlet

Lug, lag hollow
Machaire (maghera) plain
Mael, mao (mweel) bald, bare hill
Maigh plain
Mám, Madhm (maum) pass
Más long, low hill
Mór (more) big
Muing long-grassed expanse
Mullach summit
Poll hole, pond
Raibhach grey
Rinn headland
Rua, ruadh red
Scairbh (scarriff) shallow ford
Scealp rocky cleft
Sceilig (skellig) rock
Sceir (sker, pl. skerry) rock, reef (Norse)

Sescenn (seskin) marsh
Sean old
Sliabh (slieve) mountain
Sli (slee) way
Spinc pointed pinnacle
Sron nose, nose-like mountain fea~~
Sruth, sruthair, sruthán stream
Stuaic (stook) pointed pinnacle
Suí, suidhe (see) seat
Taobh, taebh (tave) side, hillside
Tír (teer) land, territory
Teach house
Tobar well
Tor tower-like rock
Torc wild boar
Tulach little hill

The reader who wants to know more about the meanings of Irish place-names should consult P. W. Joyce's great book. Originally published in 1869, it is still the most useful source of information on the subject. It has been reprinted recently (see Bibliography).

Organized walks and walking routes
Those who prefer to do their hill-walking in company may be interested in this list of the various organized annual walks. They are mostly longer than the related routes which we have described.

April
Comeragh Bog Trot (Route 8 +)

May
Maumturks Walk (Route 24 + +)
Blackstairs Walk (Route 6 +)

June
Reeks Walk (Routes 14 + 15)
Mourne Wall Walk (Routes 46, 47, 48 +)
Lugnaquillia Walk (Routes 1, 3, 5 +)

July
Circuit of Imaal Route 5 +)

September
Knockmealdowns Walk (Route 9 +)
Glover Marathon (Routes 41, 42, 43)

Information about these walks may be obtained from the Tourist Board or the FMCI.

While long-distance walking routes have not been developed to anything like the same extent in Ireland as in the rest of Europe, a start has been made with the Ulster Way, which makes a complete circuit round Northern Ireland, and the Wicklow Way, which is the beginning of a walking route all round Ireland. They are specifically designed to avoid the summits, but they do serve a useful purpose for the dedicated walker in linking many of the hill routes we have described. Further information from Cospoir, the National Sports Council, 11th Floor, Hawkins House, Dublin 2; and the Sports Council for Northern Ireland, 2A Upper Malone Road, Belfast BT9 5LA. The two field officers responsible for the walking routes, Wilfred Capper in Belfast and and J. B. Malone in Dublin, are extremely knowledgeable.

Maps

Republic of Ireland OS Maps
The largest scale up-to-date maps covering the Republic are $\frac{1}{2}''$ to 1 mile (1:126,720). They are modern and reasonably accurate, certainly in the valleys, but the scale is too small for them to be really suitable for the hill-walker. They have contours at 100-ft

intervals and are layer-tinted, so they give quite a good picture of the shape of the countryside. The contours above the 1,000-ft mark were only surveyed at 250-ft intervals, so most of the contours on the map are interpolated and their accuracy cannot be guaranteed. Woods are shown rather vaguely with tree symbols. Old tracks across the hills are shown, but may now be invisible. New forestry tracks are marked, but since they are marked from information supplied by the head office of the Forestry and Wildlife Service, rather than from the forester who actually built the tracks, they are not always accurate. With all their faults, however, these are the best available maps for most mountain areas of the Republic, and reference is made to them in each route description.

There are a few up-to-date 1″ to 1 mile (1:63,360) District maps, and as far as mountain areas are concerned, the Dublin District and Wicklow District maps cover the Wicklow Hills, and the Killarney District map covers the Reeks and the central part of the Beara peninsula. These are to be preferred to the ½″ map for their larger scale, if nothing else, but they do have drawbacks. Above the 1,000-ft level, contours are only at 250-ft intervals, so that many minor and a few major physical features do not appear. They are layer-tinted and woods are shown in green. However, a splodge of green on the map may refer to a new forestry plantation with trees still hardly visible above the heather, so be careful.

A problem common to both 1″ and ½″ maps is the delineation of crags and cliffs. This is arbitrary in the extreme. There are many unmarked crags and, on the other hand, some marked crags are easily passable. The problem is more acute on the 1″ maps, because the big contour interval masks the steepness of the ground. It would be impossible to tell from the map that Lugnaquillia, for instance (Route 5), is cliff-bound on both the north and the south.

There are pre-1914 1″ maps of the whole Republic, uncoloured, again with contours at 250-ft intervals above 1,000 ft. Because of their larger scale they have some advantages over the ½″ map, but we would not consider it worth while for hill-walkers to buy these maps normally. The sheets are small and they cost as much as the other maps (£1.10 per map at time of writing). A 1:50,000 map of Wicklow has just been published to show the line of the Wicklow

Way, replacing the old Dublin and Wicklow District sheets. But it is still based on the old survey, and though there are improvements in the marking of crags, etc, the old contour intervals remain unchanged.

In fairness to the Ordnance Survey in Dublin it must be stressed that they work on a small budget and that they have other priority surveys to carry out. A 1:100,000 map covering the country is projected, and some areas in the north, including Donegal, will be covered by the new Northern Ireland 1:50,000 series.

$\frac{1}{2}''$ and 1″ District maps are obtainable in bookshops locally, or from the Government Publications Office, GPO Arcade, Henry Street, Dublin 1. The old black-and-white 1″ map, and unfolded copies of the other maps, are only available from the Ordnance Survey Office, Phoenix Park, Dublin.

Northern Ireland OS Maps

Though the maps are much better than in the Republic, they are still worse than in Britain. There is a reasonably up-to-date 1″ to 1 mile (1:63,360) map, in exactly the same style as the 1″ District maps in the Republic, with all their disadvantages. There is no doubt, though, that these 1″ maps are much easier to read than the $\frac{1}{2}''$.

A new series of 1:50,000 (approx $1\frac{1}{4}''$ to 1 mile) metric maps, comparable to the British 1:50,000 second series, is being prepared, but so far only ten sheets have appeared. Mountaineers and ramblers look forward to the time when the series will cover, as we are promised, not only Northern Ireland, but Donegal as well. There is a newly published 1:25,000 map of the Mournes, comparable with the British maps on the same scale. This is a very fine map indeed, very clear, with crags and field-boundaries marked, and a 10-m contour interval which brings out the shape of the hills almost as well as hill-shading would. There are $\frac{1}{2}''$ to 1 mile maps of Northern Ireland published by both Ordnance Surveys, which you may like to buy because the 100-ft contours (even if only interpolated) do show the shape of the country better than those on the 1″. Most walkers in Wicklow, for instance, tend to use both maps.

1″ and $\frac{1}{2}''$ maps are obtainable locally, or from Ordnance Survey of Northern Ireland, 83 Ladas Drive, Belfast BT6 9FJ.

Other maps

There are no other maps of any significant value for walking, but
the regional Tourist Boards produce maps which show places of
tourist interest and these may also be of help in finding
accommodation. Both OS publish $\frac{1}{4}''$ (1:253,440) maps which may
be useful for navigation by car, and for identifying distant
landmarks from summit viewpoints.

Metric conversion tables

The figures in the central columns can be read as either the
metric or the British measure. Thus 1 inch = 25.4 millimetres; or 1
millimetre = 0.039 inches

Inches		Millimetres	Miles		Kilometres
0.039	1	25.4	0.621	1	1.609
0.079	2	50.8	1.243	2	3.219
0.118	3	76.2	1.864	3	4.828
0.157	4	101.6	2.486	4	6.437
0.197	5	127.0	3.107	5	8.047
0.236	6	152.4	3.728	6	9.656
0.276	7	177.8	4.350	7	11.265
0.315	8	203.2	4.971	8	12.875
0.354	9	228.6	5.592	9	14.484

Feet		Metres	Sq feet		Sq metres
3.281	1	0.305	10.764	1	0.093
6.562	2	0.610	21.528	2	0.186
9.843	3	0.914	32.292	3	0.297
13.123	4	1.219	43.056	4	0.372
16.404	5	1.524	53.820	5	0.465
19.685	6	1.829	64.583	6	0.557
22.966	7	2.134	75.347	7	0.650
26.247	8	2.438	86.111	8	0.753
29.528	9	2.743	96.875	9	0.836

Yards		Metres	Sq yards		Sq metres
1.094	1	0.914	1.196	1	0.836
2.187	2	1.829	2.392	2	1.675
3.281	3	2.743	3.588	3	2.508
4.374	4	3.658	4.784	4	3.345
5.468	5	4.572	5.980	5	4.181

Accommodation and access

Accommodation
Notes on accommodation are given for each area and the purpose of
these general remarks is simply to give the foreign visitor some idea
of what is available.

Bord Fáilte Eireann (Baggot Street Bridge, Dublin 2) for the
Republic and the Northern Ireland Tourist Board (48 High Street,
Belfast BT1 2DS) both prepare booklets listing hotels, guest
houses, caravan parks, and farmhouse accommodation. These
booklets are intended primarily for foreign tourists and are rather
easier to obtain abroad than in Ireland! They also include complete
price lists. The hill-walker will probably be looking at the cheaper
end of the scale and he or she will find, especially in the guest
houses and 'B and Bs', a friendly welcome and good value for
money.

Quite a few of the routes described can conveniently be walked
from a youth hostel. The Mournes, Wicklow, and Kerry all have
good hostel coverage. Naturally you have to be a member of a
Youth Hostel Association to use them; if you are not already a
member it is, of course, quite easy to join either An Óige (the Irish
Youth Hostel Association, 39 Mountjoy Square, Dublin 1) or
YHANI (the Youth Hostel Association of Northern Ireland, 56
Bradbury Place, Belfast BT7 IR4). You can also get handbooks
from these addresses. Irish youth hostels are all self-catering and are
mostly simple in style. Especially in the more remote areas they
tend to be fairly small and have a friendly and relaxed atmosphere.
During the summer, especially at weekends, they soon fill up, and
you are advised to book in advance (booking details are in the
handbooks).

There are not many 'official' campsites in Ireland and most of
them are geared to caravans rather than tents (some do not accept
tents). A caravan is no bad base for exploring the Irish hills, since it
is fairly easy to park it, even away from caravan parks, and, given
the Irish climate, you may find a tent a little damp. Lists of official
sites are available from the Tourist Boards.

Campers are generally welcome; obviously you should ask

permission before camping on anyone's land, but this will rarely be refused and it is unlikely that the charge will be excessive. If the price strikes you as high, move on to the next farm. I do not want to harp on the bad weather, but there is no doubt we do have wet days, even in summer, so make sure that your tent is waterproof and do not pitch it too close to a stream that may rise. Streams rise and fall equally quickly, but the quick fall will not be much consolation if you have had six inches of water in your tent.

If you are a member of a mountaineering club, you can use the Huts in Wicklow and the Mourne Mountains belonging to various Irish mountaineering clubs: details of these from the Information Officer, Federation of Mountaineering Clubs of Ireland, 20 Leopardstown Gdns, Blackrock, Co. Dublin. While clubs are very glad to welcome foreign walkers and climbers, it is essential that you book first. In addition to club huts there are a few commercial 'bunk-houses' and these have been mentioned in the appropriate place.

If you are planning a fairly static holiday you may like to rent a cottage and cook for yourself. The 'Rent an Irish Cottage' network of specially built cottages is particularly to be recommended, and several groups of cottages are well-placed for the mountaineer.

Access

There are numerous car-ferry services from Britain: Cairnryan-Larne, Stranraer-Larne, Liverpool-Dublin, Holyhead-Dun Laoire, Holyhead-Dublin, Fishguard-Rosslare, Pembroke-Rosslare, and Pembroke-Cork. There are direct services from Continental Europe: Le Havre/Cherbourg-Rosslare, and Roscoff-Cork.

The four major airports in Ireland – Belfast, Dublin, Cork, and Shannon – are well served with flights from several British airports and most major Continental airports – and also from New York, Boston, and Chicago.

Ireland is too small for there to be much in the way of internal air services, and internal public transport is, therefore, either rail or road. Information about public transport is given in the introduction to each area and the only general remark which we can make is, sadly, that public transport in most mountain areas is conspicuous by its absence. Timetables are obtainable from CIE for the Republic, and Ulsterbus for Northern Ireland. There are also a few private services.

Ireland has a good network of roads and, apart from the cities, rush hours, and the main roads to and from Dublin, Cork, and Belfast on Friday and Sunday evenings, these roads are not too crowded. So it seems to us good sense for the foreign visitor to bring a car, or hire one in Ireland. Even better, perhaps, is to hire a bicycle, which it is easy and cheap to do.

Mountain safety

The Irish hills are still relatively unfrequented. This is a happy situation for the hill-walker, except when he gets into serious trouble and needs help. There is efficient, mostly voluntary, mountain rescue for the whole country, but a rescue team may have to come from a considerable distance, so it is important to take all reasonable precautions:

1. Have plenty of warm clothing, especially wind- and rain-resistant outer garments (jacket or anorak with hood and overtrousers). Do not wear jeans; when wet and subjected to a cold wind, they are a passport to hypothermia.
2. Carry map and compass, and know how to use them. Also carry a watch, whistle, torch, small first-aid kit, a spare pullover and (for a long walk) a bivvy bag.
3. In winter be prepared for winter conditions. Especially on the 3,000-ft mountains you may well need an ice-axe.
4. Have a reserve supply of food in case of emergency.
5. Check weather forecasts. Keep a constant lookout for changes. On high ground mist and rain can close in with alarming speed.
6. Plan walks carefully. Do not over-estimate the physical capacity of yourself or other members of the party. Study routes and allow enough time to get back before dark. Check in advance for possible 'escape routes' should the weather deteriorate during the walk.

7. Always leave information about where you are going and when you will be back. Tell someone at your hotel, guest-house or hostel (there is a book for this purpose in mountain youth hostels) or leave a note in your tent or car. If you choose *not* to return to your original base, make sure someone is not calling out the rescue team for you.
8. Do not hesitate to turn back or cut a walk short if the weather deteriorates or if the route is too much for you or one of your party. 'Pressing on' is folly, not courage, and can be disastrous.
9. If you do have an accident contact the nearest police station (Gardai in the Republic, RUC in Northern Ireland), who will be able to call out a rescue team.

At the time of writing, Mountain Rescue Posts are as follows:
Northern Ireland
Newcastle RUC Station (Mournes)
Ballycastle RUC Station (Antrim)
Enniskillen RUC Station (Fermanagh)

The Republic
Ben Lettery Youth Hostel (Connemara)
Errigal Youth Hostel (Donegal)
Tiglin Adventure Centre, Ashford (Wicklow)

Mountain Rescue Teams are as follows:
Northern Ireland
RUC (Police) Mountain Rescue Team (Mournes, Northern Ireland generally and Donegal)
Mourne Mountain Rescue Team (Mournes)
NE Mountain and Cliff Rescue Team (Antrim, etc.)

The Republic
An Óige Mountain Rescue Team Dublin (Wicklow and elsewhere)
IMC Mountain Rescue Team Dublin (Wicklow and elsewhere)
SE Mountain Safety Association Team (Blackstairs, Comeraghs, Knockmealdowns and Galtees)
Kerry Mountain Rescue Association Team (Cork and Kerry)
Galway Mountain Rescue Team (Connemara)

Using the guide
It is impossible within an illustrated book of reasonable size and
cost to describe all the good walks over the Irish hills, or even all the
routes up the selected peaks. What we have tried to do is to select
the best, or sometimes the biggest or most typical peaks, in each
area and describe at least one route to the top. The photographs
have been selected for two purposes: firstly, to help you to
recognize your route; secondly, to give you an idea of the type of
scenery and terrain that you will meet in each mountain area.

We hope that this book, with its sketch-maps and photographs,
will enable you to plan your walks before you start your holiday,
and that, when you have sampled a route or two from this book,
with the aid of the OS map you will embark on other routes on
other mountains. There are a number of books which will help you
to do this, and they are listed in the Bibliography.

Time and Distance
For each route we have given the distance in miles and the height to
be climbed. From these we have deduced the time that the walk
might take you, using 'Naismith's Rule', which says that a
hill-walker of average fitness will take 1 hour for each 3 miles of
horizontal distance walked, and half an hour for each 1,000 ft of
ascent. This is very rough and ready and (apart from the abilities of
the walker) does not take into account the effects of bad weather or
difficult ground, nor of course does it include time for any halts.

So the times we have given you are only an estimate. A small, fit
party will move more quickly, a large party will take longer. We
suggest that you work out for your party your own variant of
Naismith's Rule – perhaps 2½ miles in 1 hour and 750 ft of ascent in
half an hour – and apply it to the distance and height mentioned in
the route description. You should consider also that you will be
quicker than average on a short route than a long one. (The metric
equivalent is 5 km in 1 hour and 100 m of ascent in 10 minutes.)

Place names
We have followed the OS nomenclature in all cases (even when it
differs from the popular version). Many of them are rather
unsatisfactory translations of Irish names and we have endeavoured

to give the Irish names and their meanings for important points. But please remember that because the English names are often corrupt, several meanings are possible. There is a glossary on p 30 of Irish terms for the more common features found in the hills. Quite a few mountains are without names, and in such cases we have described them, for example, as 'Pt 2,307' from the spot height at the summit, or 'Pt 2,100 contour' for the highest contour, if there is no spot height.

Grid references

All the maps mentioned above (except the old black-and-white 1″ to 1 mile) have a metric grid superimposed on them, which can be used to pinpoint (to the nearest 100 metres) any feature on the map. The grid covers the whole island. Instructions on the bottom of each sheet tell you how to use the grid. On the 1″ maps the kilometre squares are marked, and it is comparatively easy to divide these squares mentally into tenths. On the ½″ maps only 10 kilometre squares are marked and it is useful to provide yourself with a romer (a home-made card one will do) for map references on this scale.

Map references have been used to locate the start of each route described, and elsewhere as necessary. The reference letter has been omitted, since the nearest identical reference is 100 kms away. Map references used in the text are six-figure, are preceded by the letters 'MR', and are in brackets.

Maps in the book

The sketch maps in the book are designed to show the routes. They are NOT a substitute for the relevant Ordnance Map, especially as they only have approximate contours at 500-ft intervals. They do have a number of names on them which are not on the OS map, but which are mentioned in the text. The sketch maps also show crags and woods, even if these are not on the OS maps, though naturally they are only approximate.

Navigation

There are very few paths on the Irish hills and it is essential that you carry a map and compass and are competent to use both. Most of

the hills are rounded and if a mist comes down – unfortunately this
is not uncommon – without a compass you will be completely lost.

Revision of information
Inevitably, some of the information in this guidebook will become
out dated; this is particularly true of useful addresses and
publications. Each year, Bord Fáilte Eireann publishes free
information sheets, *Hill-walking and rock-climbing* and *Long
distance walking routes*, which are well worth obtaining.

   If you do find errors in this book, the Federation of
Mountaineering Clubs of Ireland will be glad to know about them
(see address in 'Accommodation and access' section).

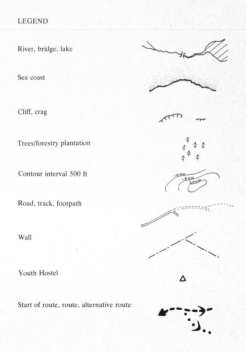

LEGEND

River, bridge, lake

Sea coast

Cliff, crag

Trees/forestry plantation

Contour interval 500 ft

Road, track, footpath

Wall

Youth Hostel

Start of route, route, alternative route

The granite mountains of the east

South of Dublin lies the long hump of granite that forms the
Wicklow Mountains. Typically, the summits of these hills are
rounded domes of granite or schist, boggy, and not overly exciting
for walking. But below the rounded tops are fine glacial corries,
steep-sided lake-filled valleys, and fine waterfalls. We have chosen
five routes which combine good scenery and good walking.
However, these five routes only scratch the surface of Wicklow
walking, and we have had to leave out many good routes – the big
hump of Mullaghcleevaun overlooking Poulaphouca reservoir,
Djouce and Powerscourt Waterfall, the Three Rock and its
neighbours that overlook the streets of Dublin, the
beautifully-shaped quartzite Sugarloaf which, standing isolated to
the east, offers magnificent views of the main ridge. The finest walk
in Wicklow, of course, is the 'Lug Walk', which follows the main
ridge from Corrig (see Route 1) to Lugnaquillia (Route 5), in all 33
miles and 7,500 ft of ascent.

The granite continues down into Wexford, rising again to form
Mount Leinster and the Blackstairs Mountains, which provide our
sixth route in the east.

Bus services
In Wicklow these are quite comprehensive. There are CIE services
down the west side of the range to Blessington, Baltinglass and
beyond (for Mount Leinster). There are a number of local services
to the north end of the range. On the east a CIE service via Wicklow
serves Rathdrum and the region beyond; while the privately run St
Kevin's bus goes to Glendalough (Routes 2, 3 and 4) – phone
Dublin 818119 for details.

Car access
The main road (N81) down the west side of the range will bring you
to Annalecky crossroads, where you turn left for Donard and
Lugnaquillia (Route 5), or further south to Bunclody, from whence

you can head west towards Mount Leinster (Route 6). There are a
variety of access roads to the east of the hills. You can take the main
road through Bray (N11) to Kilmacanogue where you turn right on
to the T61 to Glendalough. Routes 2, 3, and 4 are all reached from
this road. An alternative approach from Dublin is along the T43
through The Scalp, (a spectacular rocky-sided overflow channel),
the small town of Enniskerry and along the old coach road, joining
the T61 at Roundwood. Running right through the middle of the
hills is the Military Road, L94, built by the British after the 1798
rebellion.

Accommodation
Wicklow is one of the few areas that has a network of youth hostels
within walking distance of each other. Glencree Hostel is a possible
base for Route 1, Glendalough Hostel is a good centre for Routes 3
and 4, and Ballinclea is the normal starting point for Lugnaquillia
(Route 5). There are two Mountaineering Club huts in Glendasan,
near Glendalough.

Maps
$\frac{1}{2}''$ sheet 16 covers the Wicklow Mountains and sheet 19 shows
Mount Leinster and the Blackstairs. There are 1″ 'District' maps of
Dublin (as far south as Kippure and Glencree) and Wicklow (from
Kippure to Lugnaquillia). Both these maps have been superseded
by the 1:50,000 map that the Ordnance Survey has produced to
show the Wicklow Way. This map, unfortunately, is based on the
old survey, and still only has contours at 250-ft intervals above
1,000 ft, but some additional information has been incorporated.

1 Kippure and Glenasmole
It is comforting to know that you can emerge from the city of
Dublin and find yourself, after a few short miles, in an area as bleak
and lonely as the city is man-made and crowded (plate 1). Maybe
Upper Glenasmole, which forms the focal point of this walk, is a
little *too* bleak and featureless, but on fine days with the skylark
overhead and the dried-out bog beneath your feet, it's as pleasant a

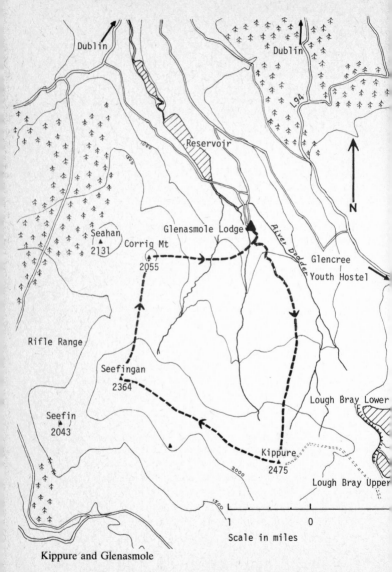

Kippure and Glenasmole

1 Lower Lough Bray, with the ridge of Kippure behind

spot as you'll find anywhere. (We'll say nothing about wet winter days!)

To get there, drive into Glenasmole (*Gleann na smól*, valley of the thrush) taking the road along the western side of the reservoir. After crossing the major bridge at the south-east end take the first turn right and park at the hairpin bend (MR 110197). There is room to park one or two cars only. Or the No 49A bus will leave you about ½ mile short of the reservoir.

Pass through the gate on the bend and walk up the track past Glenasmole Lodge on the left. The track will lead you gently upwards towards Kippure (2,475 ft, *Ciop mhor*, big place of the mountain grass), whose summit is clearly (too clearly) marked by a TV transmitter. As you ascend, you may like to glance behind you to see the reservoir opening up gradually (plate 2), and also the narrow valley of the Cot Brook to the west. When, after about 1

2 Looking north down Glenasmole from the slopes of Kippure, with Bohernabreena Reservoir in the background

mile, the track swings sharp right and begins to drop towards this valley, you bid it a fond farewell, and take to the bog and the long slow ascent to Kippure. The ground from here to Kippure is generally wet and boggy, enlivened by rough peat-hags in the later stages.

From Kippure the route runs along a broad wet ridge north-west to Seefingan (2,364 ft). Southward lies the youthful River Liffey and beyond it the Coronation Plantation and the Cleevaun range. A useful aid to navigation along this rather desolate stretch is the ditch which runs from the saddle point up on to Seefingan. The broad level summit of this peak is marked on its western edge by a large passage grave. It has not been excavated, unlike the similar one crowning Seefin to the south-west.

Heading north towards Corrig, the route drops over rough

ground to the saddle at Barnacreel. Along here there are glimpses
of Sugarloaf to the east, its distinctive cone looking out of place in a
range of gentle contours. This part of the route runs along the
county boundary; coincidentally, it is the boundary of the
rifle-range, and there is a useful line of 'WD' pillars to mark the
latter. One such pillar marks the summit of Corrig (2,055 ft), which
shows none of the rocks from which it presumably derives its name.

Walk down over rough ground in a north-easterly direction off
Corrig towards a fence running south-west to north-east on the far
side of the Slade Brook. On this stretch a single tree about half-way
down is a useful landmark. About opposite the fence cross the
narrow steep-sided valley of the Slade Brook and, once across, walk
with the fence on your left. Turn right at the corner of the fence and
follow a small path which leads to a wall and the end of a fence.
Keep to the right of this fence down to the Cot Brook. Once across
this stream, turn left and follow the bank down to yet another fence.
Follow this down to the track which began the route earlier in the
day. From here return directly to the car.

This route is 7½ miles long, with a climb of 2,200 ft, and the
Naismith time for it is 3¾ hours, excluding halts.

Maps: ½" sheet 16; 1" Dublin District; 1:50,000 Wicklow Way.

2 Around Lough Tay and Lough Dan

'Short but sweet' describes this route – but the few hours that it
takes encompass some of the most majestic areas in Wicklow with a
beauty reminiscent, in its combination of valley, lake, and towering
mountains, of the Lake District. Perhaps parts of it are a little too
'chocolate-box', but if it is scenery you want, this walk is excellent.

To reach the start, take the Sally Gap Road (L161) for about 1¼
miles west from Anna Carter Crossroads on the T61. At this point
you will pass a small gate on the left and almost immediately
afterwards a larger gate between two large stone pillars (MR
172065). A noticeboard here specifies the distance to Lough Dan in
Irish miles – whether to bewilder or encourage (Irish miles being
longer than statute) is not known! From this point you can admire
your first objective. Fancy lies across the valley to the west, its

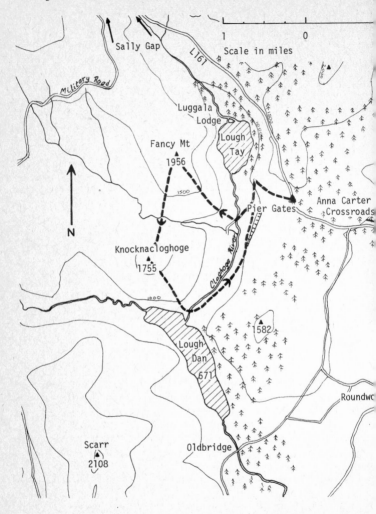

Lough Tay and Lough Dan

3 Lough Tay, with the cliffs of Luggala behind it

towering cliffs (well-known to climbers as Luggala) hanging above heart-shaped Lough Tay (plate 3). Surely a memorable sight! Further to the south lies your second peak, Knocknacloghoge, further down the Cloghoge (*Cloghóg*, stony land) Valley (plate 4).

Take the tarmacadam road (cars *not* allowed) through the large stone pillars as far as a bridge over the turbulent Cloghoge River. Just beyond the bridge turn right on to a track and follow it to where there is a corner of a stone wall on the right. Turn right here to follow the wall until you meet a bank across your path. Beyond the bank there are two part-banks part-walls, running west. Follow the right one uphill. It peters out after some distance but you must persevere to the top of Fancy (1,956 ft, perhaps *Fuinnse*, ash tree) –

4 Looking down the Cloghoge River towards Lough Dan. The slopes of Fancy Mt are on the right, with the summit of Knocknacloghoge right centre

a strenuous but rewarding climb, with lovely views unfolding all the way.

However, I am always a little disappointed by the top of Fancy itself – it promises so much scenically, only to deceive at the summit, rather like Benbulbin in Co. Sligo. The whole western aspect reveals a dull flat bogland and much of the eastern views are hidden. There isn't even a clear-cut top or cairn to mark the summit.

Leaving Fancy, drop southwards over rough terrain to the Cloghoge Brook. Cross it – you may have to detour upstream after wet weather – and ascend the opposite bank to the cairn at the top of Knocknacloghoge. From there you can admire Lough Dan with the Carrigvore-Mullaghcleevaun-Tonelagee ridge forming an arc from north to south-west.

From this point you may need a compass bearing to reach your next objective, the two-story house situated at the point where the Cloghoge River enters Lough Dan. Cross the stepping-stones beside the house and turn left on to a path. This will take you up the side of the picturesque Cloghoge River and eventually out on to the road you started on. Turn right here, and walk steeply uphill to the car.

This route is 6 miles long, with 2,400 ft of ascent, and should take about 3½ hours' walking time.

Note: The Guinness family house is set at the head of Lough Tay. While the owners do not object to walkers on the hills, they not unreasonably do not want them near the house.

Maps: ½″ sheet 16; 1″ Wicklow District; 1:50,000 Wicklow Way.

3 Tonelagee

This is a short high-level route starting more than 1,000 ft up in the heart of the range. There are no serious navigational problems. The terrain towards the end of the route is difficult, with high heather and frequent undulations – otherwise it is fairly easy. One point worth noting is that the Glenmacnass River (*Gleann luig an easa*, glen of the hollow of the waterfall) must be forded right at the start of the walk and again at the end. After heavy rain it may be impassable.

The route starts at Glenmacnass car-park (MR 115029). This car-park can conveniently be reached from either direction on the Military Road. The road from the south is a steep uphill from Laragh passing the spectacular Glenmacnass Waterfall (plate 5) on the left just before the car-park, also on the left. From the north, there are 6½ miles of rather featureless high-level bogland south of Sally Gap before reaching the car-park on the right. The car-park itself is commodious and unmistakable.

Cross the Glenmacnass River just downstream from the car-park. As noted above, it may prove difficult to cross. Once across climb up beside the forest, along a ditch and follow the broad ridge uphill keeping to its right (northern) side until Lough Ouler (*Loch iolar*, eagle lake), the large corrie lake at the foot of Tonelagee, comes

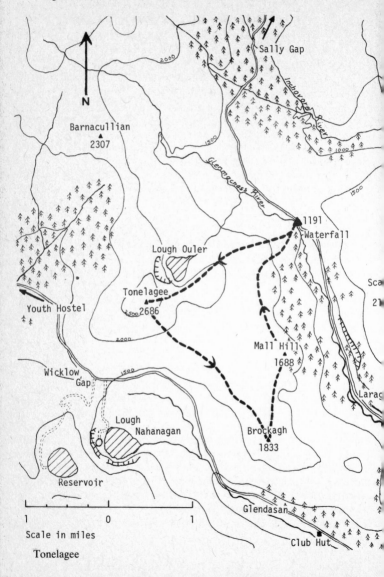

Tonelagee

5 The Glenmacnass Waterfall

into view. Then aim for the high ground at the southern end of the
lake, before tackling the last 700 ft to the summit. The views around
the lake are spectacular: the dark waters of the heart-shaped lake
itself, the great triangle of cliffs rising sheer from the lake, and the
contrasting vegetated slopes to the left. The gullies of these slopes
may be tackled by the sure-footed, instead of the easier rock-strewn
slopes further south.

From the summit of Tonelagee (2,686 ft, *Tóin le gaoth*, backside
to the wind, plate 6), marked by a trig pillar, head south-east along
the south-western side of the ridge which is wedged in the angle
formed by Glenmacnass and Glendasan. You will notice three
subdued summits ahead to the right of a flat, wet, river valley
containing a tiny lake not marked on the map. Your target, about $2\frac{1}{4}$
miles off, is the furthest of these – Brockagh (1,833 ft). It is a walk
over undulating featureless terrain which nevertheless offers good
views down into lonely Glendasan on the right. Brockagh itself,
crowned by a tiny cairn, is unexciting.

6 The summit of Tonelagee in winter, with Mullaghcleevaun in the background

From here it is homeward bound. Contouring round the edge of a rock-strewn ridge, rather than dropping into the valley, push north-east to Mall Hill, a shoulder more than a peak. A line of old forest fence posts leads northwards from here. After following these for a short distance it is advisable to contour along the hillside across a stretch of high and difficult heather, rather than slavishly following the edge of the forest. Where the forest veers to the right continue straight ahead to cross a small river. To follow the forest here leads to tiring ground and an unnecessary climb out of a river valley. When directly opposite Kanturk Mountain, the shoulder of Scarr (marked on the OS 1″ map as a 1500-ft contour line), a drop to the right should lead down the side of the forest to Glenmacnass River and the car-park.

The total length of the walk is 7 miles, with a climb of 1,800 ft, and it will take about 3½ hours, excluding halts.

Maps: ½″ sheet 16; 1″ Wicklow District; 1:50,000 Wicklow Way.

4 Mullacor and Derrybawn

This is surely one of the most dramatic and memorable walks in Wicklow – a short but energetic route with some of the finest scenery in the range to entice the faint-hearted. There are some sections, particularly at the start, requiring care to avoid navigational errors, but most of the rest is plain sailing.

The start is at the Upper car-park at Glendalough (*Gleann dá loch*, glen of the two lakes, MR 112964). Do not confuse this with the car-park on the river just past the Royal Hotel. This one is about ¾ mile further on to the east of the Upper Lake.

From the car-park you can see your first goal, the craggy and imposing wooded promontory rising high above the southern side of the lake. It is possible to tackle it directly but it is a tough scramble. Instead you should take it by stealth. Cross the grassy sward to the south of the car-park and take the bridge beyond with the signpost indicating *Poll an Easa* (pool of the waterfall). Branch left at the fork to follow the course of the tumbling Lugduff Brook as it plunges in a narrow defile into Glendalough. Rejoin the main forest track and walk to the multiple junction a little way beyond. Fork right here on to the track signposted 'Prison Rock Walk' but note the left fork beyond at this junction – with any luck you will be trudging down this path later in the day.

Walk up the Prison Rock Walk. A hundred yards or so beyond the first bend, a left one, you will see a fence heading sharply uphill on the right. Follow the path on the right of the fence. It is a sharp climb but you can console yourself with the thought that most of the navigational problems are now over.

Near the top of the hill, cross the fence at the first stile and then cross another stile a few yards further on. You have now emerged at the top of the Spink (*Spinc*, pointed hill) with the Upper Lake seemingly at your feet (plate 7) and the high massive wall of Camaderry and its popular climbing crag beyond it. While resting, note the position of this last stile carefully. If you ever attempt this route in the reverse direction, this is where you will have to branch right to avoid a precipitous descent over the end of the Spink.

The next few miles are easily described. Simply turn left and head west and upwards along the clear path with forest to the left and on

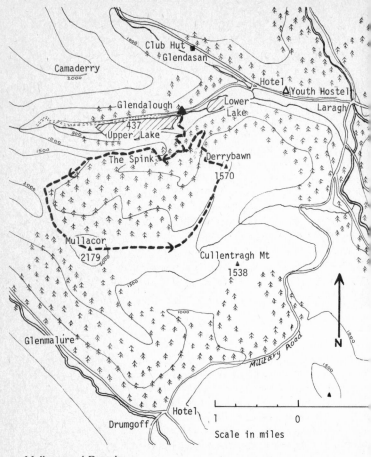

The following labels appear on the map:

Club Hut
Glendasan
Camaderry
2000
Hotel
Youth Hostel
Glendalough
437
Upper Lake
Lower Lake
Laragh
The Spink
Derrybawn
1570
Mullacor
2179
Cullentragh Mt
1538
Glenmalure
Military Road
N
Hotel
Drumgoff
1   0
Scale in miles

Mullacor and Derrybawn

7 Descending the Spink from Lugduff, with Glendalough and the Upper and Lower lakes below

the right the magnificent glacial valley of Glendalough. It is a truly beautiful walk. After a mile or so the path bends south-west away from Glendalough and the views deteriorate a little. Continue along this path with the fence on your left, over two stiles, to the crest of the Lugduff-Mullacor ridge at a place called Lodarrig, about 2 miles from your emergence on the Spink. You will recognize this point because the fence changes direction and there is a stile set into it on the angle. Cross this stile and head south-east up the imposing grassy bulk to the top of Mullacor (*Mullach mhór* big summit). At 2,179 ft you are now at the highest point of the walk.

From Mullacor continue east about 1 mile along the broad ridge with forest on your left. The forest edge then swings sharply north

8 On the Derrybawn ridge, looking north. In the distance can be seen (left to right) Scarr, Djouce, and the Sugarloaf

but you continue on the same bearing towards the hump-backed Derrybawn Ridge (plate 8), an unmistakable rib of bare metamorphic rock. You will note that the 1″ OS map gives little indication of its shape. Walk along this ridge for about 1 mile to the first cairn, a small one, marking the summit of Derrybawn (1,570 ft, *Doire ban*, white oakwood).

At this point a little care is needed. You have to hit the shallow 'V' formed by the forest edge where there is a path through the trees. If you miss it, you may find yourself floundering through dense forest. So head due west through high heather to the forest edge. Turn right here and follow the forest edge to the 'V', only a few hundred yards distant. As an additional point of identification there is a single deciduous tree here, the only one in the vicinity.

Safely at the 'V', climb the fence and descend steeply to the forest track. Turn right here and branch left at the first T-junction. This will lead you down to the multiple junction encountered at the start of the walk. Retrace your steps to the car-park.

There is a climb of 1,800 ft, over 7 miles, thus giving a Naismith time for the route of 3½ hours.

Maps: ½″ sheet 16; 1″ Wicklow District; 1:50,000 Wicklow Way.

5 Lugnaquillia and the circuit of Imaal

This is a most interesting route, taking in Lugnaquillia (plate 9), the highest mountain in Wicklow. There are many spectacular views on the walk with an opportunity, under clear skies, to see all the peaks on the route from nearly every vantage point. But be warned: walk it at a fast pace or else choose a long summer day, for it will take almost 6 hours without stops. However there is an escape route about two-thirds along. Another point to remember is that you will need two cars for this walk, unless you are prepared for a 5-mile road walk back. If you do not have a car you will have to walk from Annalecky crossroads, though there are rare buses to Donard.

To get to the start, drive to Donard in the Glen of Imaal (*Gleann uí mháil*, glen of the tribe). From the village take the Ballinclea road to the youth hostel (MR 961952) where one car must be parked. Just beyond the hostel turn right for Knockanarrigan. From this village take the Aughavannagh road (marked on signpost) to Ballinfoyle, a road junction on the saddle between Ballineddan and Keadeen mountains and about 2½ miles from Knockanarrigan (MR 987902).

Park your car at the junction at Ballinfoyle and walk about 100 yards south along the road. Leave the road at the gate on the left and follow the track, which peters out after a while. Continue upwards to the summit of Ballineddan (2,151 ft, *Baile an fheadáin*, homestead of the little stream) while the wooded eastern shoulder of Keadeen opens up behind. You will find a small cairn on the rather undistinguished summit.

From Ballineddan your way lies over a broad ridge towards your next objective, Slievemaan. There is a path of sorts along this stretch but it is not always apparent. From the summit of Slievemaan (2,501 ft, *Sliabh meadhán*, middle mountain) the bulky

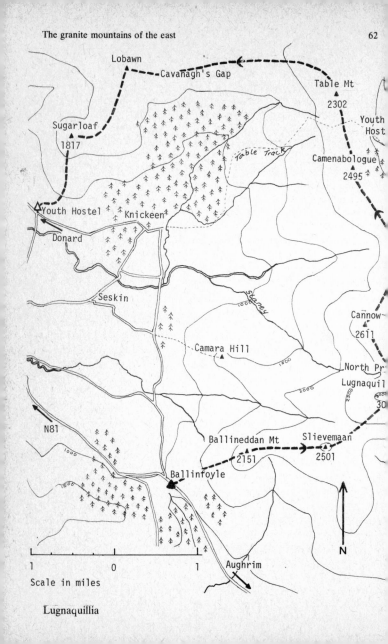

Lugnaquillia

Lugnaquillia massif looms imposingly ahead to the north-east. To reach it, you can take a direct bearing on which you will encounter a short wet section which marks the source of the Little Slaney River. Beyond it the summit of Lugnaquillia (3,039 ft, *Log an coille*, hollow of the cocks) is reached after a steep climb over rocky ground.

The summit of Lugnaquillia (plate 10), if 'summit' is the correct word, consists of a large plateau of short grass in the centre of which stands a huge cairn, which can, nonetheless, be difficult to find in bad visibility. There are no views from the cairn, but it is necessary only to walk out to the edge of the plateau for spectacular views in all directions. The views over the North and South Prisons are particularly good.

From Lugnaquillia descend northwards, keeping the forbidding North Prison on your left (the Prison is very popular for winter snow- and ice-climbing). There is pleasant terrain of short grass to Cannow, which is more a shoulder than a peak, and may be

9 Lugnaquillia from the west (Camara Hill). The summit is on the right, with the North Prison in shadow below it

10 The summit plateau of Lugnaquillia and the South Prison, in winter, from the east

11 Glenmalure. The Barravore cliffs are on the left, Camenabologue centre background, with the pass to Imaal to the right

bypassed without loss. Further down descend over the Cannow ridge to Camenabologue. There is an intermittent path along this stretch, but it is winding and not easy to follow. Be wary along this part of the route as it is only too easy to make an inadvertent descent into Glenmalure to the east.

Camenabologue (2,495 ft, *Céim na mBullóg*, pass of the bullocks) is marked by a mass of stones, some of which have been used to form a sizeable cairn. From it, there is only ½ mile to the top of the Table Track, which leads from Glenmalure (plate 11) to the Glen of Imaal. So here at the track you have to make a decision: whether to turn left and follow the track right back to the road at Knickeen, about 1½ miles from the car at Ballinclea, or whether to press on along the hills north of the Glen of Imaal. Assuming you are still fit and enthusiastic, push on the few hundred yards to Table, an aptly named 'mountain' which consists simply of a cairn (2,302 ft) set in a sea of black bog. From here your navigational problems are almost over because you can follow a wide cutting all the way to Cavanagh's Gap and Lobawn. Look out for the boundary stones along this cutting. They mark the original boundary of the Glen of Imaal artillery range, the 'WD' cut into the stones standing for 'War Department'. If they had been erected in these more euphemistic days they would be titled 'DD' for Department of Defence. What's in a name? Nothing much in this particular case, anyway.

One of these pillars marks the summit of Lobawn (2,097 ft, *Lúbán*, little bend), from which there are good views into wooded Imaal and northwards to Poulaphouca Reservoir. From here descend southwards along the ridge to Pt 1,913 and hence to Sugarloaf (which is no relation to the more famous Sugar Loaf near Bray). Head southwards again along a spur to a fence which you keep on your left. Ballinclea Youth Hostel, a large white building, will soon become visible as you descend. The best way to reach it is to keep an avenue of tall trees on your right and to enter the grounds by a gate at the rear.

The route is 12 miles long, with 3,400 ft of ascent, and will take 6 hours, excluding halts.

Note: The head of the Glen of Imaal is an artillery range. The route described keeps clear of the range, but the 'escape route' down the Table Track crosses Army property. If there is no flag flying it is safe to follow the track, though naturally you should not pick up or touch any metal object you may see.

Maps: ½" sheet 16; 1" Wicklow District; 1:50,000 Wicklow Way.

6 Mount Leinster and the Blackstairs

This splendid granite ridge extends south-westwards from the Wicklow massif and dominates the scenery in South Leinster. The ridge is well defined, though broad, and offers superb prospects. A traverse from south to north is the most rewarding expedition. This can conveniently be broken mid-way at the Sculloge Gap (638 ft) which carries the Ballymurphy-Kiltealy Road (L30). Of the two segments, the southernmost offers the most interest.

Approach either from Bunclody over the Sculloge Gap, or from Borris in the Barrow Valley, go through the village of Ballymurphy and take a lane leading south-east. Park the car at MR 791450, and pick up the cart track which leads gently upwards in a southerly direction to the col at 1,228 ft. This massive zigzag leads easily through bracken-clad slopes and is preferable to the more direct approach from Gowlin. This green road, one of the communication lines between Carlow and Wexford, was negotiated by horse and cart, and carried trade goods and beasts, establishing and maintaining family ties.

Keep to the upper track at the junction, and soon the col and the boundary of the young forest plantation on the eastern slopes of Carrigalachan will be reached.

From the col head upwards along the ridge in a north-easterly direction, ascending on fairly large scree boulders. In late July the small dark bilberry (*fraughan*) is plentiful here, providing an astringent mouthful and an excuse to pause. Indeed the last Sunday of July was known locally as Mountain Sunday and provided one of the longest-lasting popular assemblies. These have been described by Maire MacNeill as a survival of the Celtic festival of Lughnasa, celebrating the beginning of the harvest. The first potatoes of the year were dug for early dinner and eaten with bacon and white cabbage, after which the country people climbed to the meeting

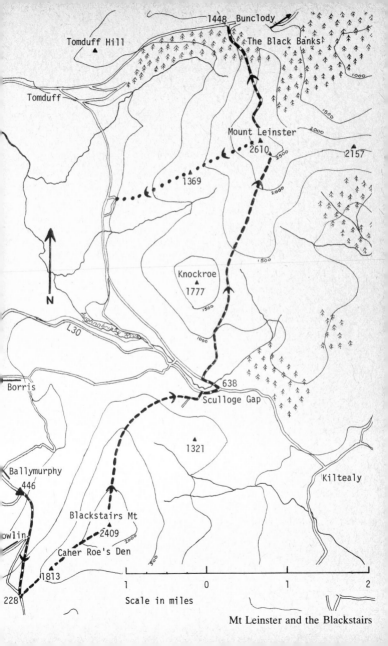

Mt Leinster and the Blackstairs

12 Ascending the final slopes of Blackstairs Mt. On the intermediate summit is Caher Roe's Den, and beyond it is Carrigalachan

place on the summit. Music, dancing, match-making, and story-telling filled the day.

The crest of the ridge, when gained, is well defined and provides easy going. The occasional outcrops, when surmounted, give excellent vantage points for a survey of the ridge ahead and the surrounding countryside. To the north-west the deeply incised Barrow Valley delineates the Castlecomer plateau and also separates out the beautiful Brandon Hill (1,703 ft). Further south still Waterford Harbour can be seen, leading to the Atlantic. Indeed the ¼″ OS Ireland South-East and a pair of binoculars will be necessary to inform the viewer, so extensive is the panorama.

A substantial granite outcrop, Caher Roe's Den, at 2,000 ft, will bring you almost opposite your starting point. Westward the field

13 View to the north-west across the Sculloge Gap to Mt Leinster

patterns and settlements are well displayed, whilst to the east are
the Slaney Valley and the Irish Sea coastline where Wexford
Harbour and the Great Saltee Island may be seen. The person
associated with Caher Roe's Den is Cathaoir na gCapall of the
O'Dempsey family in Leix. The family lands being forfeit in the
seventeenth century, he turned rapparee and controlled a large
organization which stole horses from the new-planted gentry and
sold them at distant fairs. He was hanged at Maryboro in August
1735. The Den is supposed to hold his treasure, but the entrance
has been blocked to prevent sheep getting lost.

The summit of Blackstairs Mountain (2,409 ft, plate 12) is peaty,
but gives new prospects northwards to Mount Leinster and its
eastern ridge to Black Rock Mountain. The significance of the term

'massif' as applied to the Wicklow Mountains can now be appreciated. Tara Hill (833 ft) near Courtown, and Croghan Mountain, are easy to identify, but careful study of the $\frac{1}{2}''$ map will be needed to distinguish all but the outliers.

Descend northwards along the ridge and when the slope eases, at about 1,500 ft, select a line to bring you to the high point of the Sculloge Gap where the roads join at 638 ft. Take care when descending the final section, as bracken may cover gaps between boulders. A narrow sunken lane, which you may be lucky enough to find, leads through the valley fields to the road.

For the northern segment of the ridge, take the side road leading west and north from the Gap. A laneway (MR 825478) leads north to pass a few farms and gains the moorland. Follow the track to the saddle (1,450 ft) between Knockroe (1,777 ft) with its Holy Year cross and Mount Leinster (2,610 ft, plate 13). Leave the track here and head north along the ridge, with bad peat erosion in parts, to gain the summit, which is endowed with a TV transmitting mast. Magnificent views in all directions provide a fitting reward.

Descent can be made by the tarmac service road, which leads to the Borris-Bunclody road on the col at 1,448 ft (MR 817477).

As described, the walk is 11½ miles long, with 4,200 ft of ascent, and will take a good 6 hours excluding halts. However, you still have to get back to your car! An alternative descent over Pt 1,369 to a small loopway of road (MR 800507) will save a few miles. Or you could split the walk at the Sculloge Gap.

Map: $\frac{1}{2}''$ sheet 19.

The sandstone mountains of the south-east

Many people are inclined to overlook these hills, thinking of the south-east of Ireland primarily as good agricultural land. While this is true, nearly one-third of the area can be classified as upland and one of Ireland's rare 3,000-ft mountains is to be found here.

Unlike the igneous Wicklow Mountains, these hills are all sedimentary – sandstone or conglomerate. The first range we come to, as we move south-west from the Blackstairs, is the Comeraghs (Routes 7 and 8) and their southward extension, the Monavullaghs, extending from Clonmel nearly to Dungarvan. These conglomerate hills form a boggy plateau, but the edges of the platform are cut away sharply into steep-sided rocky coums, many of them lake-filled. Lying to the west are the Knockmealdowns (Route 9), an east-west range of rounded summits with regular slopes in sharp contrast to the Comeraghs. Paralleling the Knockmealdowns is the highest range in the area, the Galtees, a fine row of peaks culminating in Galtymore, 3,018 ft (Route 10). These are fine walking hills, not too wet underfoot and, besides the walk we describe, the complete ridge makes a wonderful and not too strenuous day.

Further north are two more mountain areas, rising out of the central plain – the Slieve Felim/Silvermine group (Route 11) and the Slieve Blooms.

Train and Bus Services
The area is quite well served by the Waterford-Limerick Junction railway line, and there are buses from Dublin to Cahir, Clonmel, Mitchelstown and Tipperary Town. There are also local services which will take you to most of the likely starting places for walks, but at best there will be one bus a day in each direction, and at worst one a week.

Car Access
The main road from Dublin to Cork (N8) runs through the middle

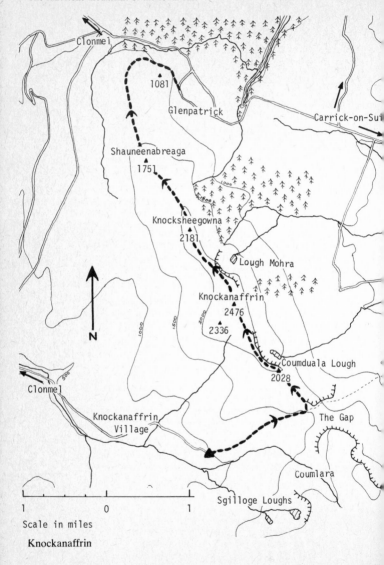

Knockanaffrin

of our area, from Cahir to Mitchelstown, passing between the Galtees and the Knockmealdowns. The north side of the Galtees can be reached by following the N24 from Cahir, and there is a wonderful road (L34) crossing the Knockmealdowns and descending to Lismore (if you have not time to walk the Knockmealdowns, at least drive over the Gap – preferably from south to north). The N72 between Dungarvan and Fermoy gives access to the Monavullaghs and Knockmealdowns from the south, and the T56 from Dungarvan to Carrick-on-Suir opens up the east side of the Comeraghs.

The Silvermine range is best approached from the Limerick–Dublin road (N7) on the north, or the T19 running through the hills from Limerick to Thurles.

Accommodation
There are three youth hostels – Lismore to the south and Ballydavid Wood and Mountain Lodge in the Galtees. Mountain Lodge *must* be visited. It is an old converted shooting-lodge, set in a wood on the south slopes of the Galtees, with superb views.

Maps
The Comeraghs and Knockmealdowns are on ½″ sheet 22. The Galtees, maddeningly, are on the joint between ½″ sheets 18 and 22. Keeper Hill is on sheet 18. There is no modern 1″, and just to further frustrate you the sheet lines of the old 1″ map also bisect the Galtees.

7 **Knockanaffrin** (Comeragh Mountains)
The spiky northern ridge of the Comeragh Mountains is a most challenging prospect when seen from any of the roads approaching the area. In practice, it turns out to be a pleasant excursion with minimal route-finding problems and there are many opportunities for easy scrambling among the rocks all along the crest.

Drive to the village of Ballymacarby on the main Clonmel-Dungarvan road (T27) and turn east on the minor road signposted to the Nire Valley. This road follows the river about 5

14 The Knockanaffrin ridge from the south-east. The track across The Gap can just be seen in the shadow

miles up the valley to where a large lay-by makes an ideal place to start the walk (MR 279126).

Follow the clearly-defined bridle path heading east towards The Gap, which effectively divides the northern ridge from the main Comeragh plateau. Across the valley to the right can be seen the western corries of Coumlara, Sgilloge, Coumalocha and Coumfea, the last three containing attractive lakes and all surrounded by majestic cliffs. Shortly before the head of The Gap is reached, at about 1,600 ft, turn left and head up the fairly steep heather-covered hillside towards a rock outcrop which marks the southern end of the ridge proper (plate 14). From here the route follows a series of tors which skirt the edge of the tremendous cliffs overlooking Coumduala (hollow of the black cliffs) on the right, and continues to ascend towards the soaring pinnacled summit of

Knockanaffrin (2,478 ft, *Cnoc an Aifrinn*, hill of the Mass). The views from this peak are exciting with the rounded dome of Slievenamon (2,368 ft, *Sliabh na mBan*, mountain of the women) prominent to the north above the forests of the Suir Valley, and the crags over Crotty's Lake standing out clearly on the eastern edge of the central plateau. To the west there is a gentle slope leading down to flattish moorland, which is crossed by two roads running almost side by side and where turf cutting is extensively carried out. To the east, beyond the forests which clothe this steep side of the ridge, is the fertile Rathgormuck plateau, once as hilly as the rest of this area but at some point in time proving so susceptible to erosion that only a northern escarpment overlooking the Suir remains.

The route continues to the north, staying close to the edge of cliffs on your right and passing a series of interesting rocky tors culminating in Knocksheegowna (2,181 ft, hill of the fairy calves). (The connection here is with the lake below you on your right, Lough Mohra, which is reputed to be the home of a herd of milk-white cows tended by a young fair-haired girl.) Past this summit the ridge swings to the left slightly and begins to descend past more outcrops until the quaintly named Shauneenabreaga (1,751 ft, little false end) is reached. This is the last of the rocks, and you are now confronted by moorland which can be crossed most easily by bearing right and heading north-east, to emerge on the minor road just west of Glenpatrick crossroads.

Apart from the initial climb to the ridge and the descent across the moor, the ground underfoot is excellent, with plenty of low grass between the rocks.

The walk is about 7 miles long, with 1,800 ft of ascent, and should take about 3½ hours without stops.

Map: ½″ sheet 22.

8 Coumshingaun and Fauscoum (Comeragh Mountains)

This climb involves traverses of the ridges on both sides of Coumshingaun, and also covers much of the Comeragh plateau. The initial section includes perhaps the nearest approach to true ridge-scrambling found in this part of the country, and in adverse conditions would be better avoided by inexperienced walkers.

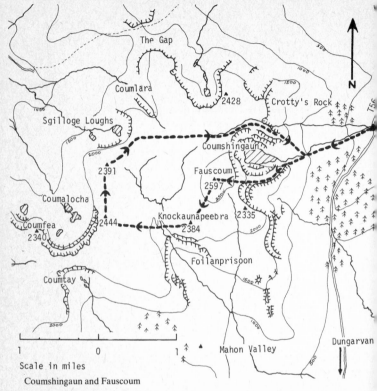

Coumshingaun and Fauscoum

The best starting point is close to the bridge and road junction to
the east of Coumshingaun (MR 349114) on the Carrick-on-Suir to
Dungarvan road (T56). Park close to a modern bungalow and then
head due west across the fields towards a massive boulder deposited
by ice millions of years ago.

Beyond the fields is the terminal moraine, and the route
continues upwards through deep bracken and boulders until you
reach the long oval-shaped lake backed by the tremendous cliffs
which dominate this famous corrie (plate 15).

15 Coumshingaun in winter

16 The Comeragh Mts from near Mahon's Bridge

At this point bear left, and begin the steep climb towards the pinnacle of rocks which stand out at the end of the southern arm of Coumshingaun (corrie of the ants) and which lead to a couple of hundred yards of mild but enjoyable ridge-scrambling. There follows a short climb on grass, and then the route continues along an arête where the tremendous drop on your right should be bypassed with care. It is possible here to look almost vertically down into either of the two corries, lake-filled Coumshingaun to the north and dry Fauscoum to the south, before tackling the final section of the ridge. This is a narrow spur which leads sharply up to the main plateau, and though it is fairly exposed there are plenty of hand- and foot-holds if you avoid the rocks by keeping slightly to the left.

Once on the plateau, continue due west up a slight slope through wind-scoured turf banks and you will soon arrive at the highest part of the range, Fauscoum (2,597 ft, wild corrie), marked only by a tiny pile of stones easily missed in bad weather. This central section of the Comeraghs is in fact shaped rather like a saucer tilted to the south-east where most of the streams drain into the Mahon River. Just north of the spot where this river tumbles over the plateau's edge is Knockaunapeebra (2,384 ft, little hill of the piper) and it is to this double-cairned peak that you should now head, for it gives a superb view over the Mahon Valley (plate 16) towards the southern coastline.

Now turn sharply downhill to the west and cross the river just above the falls, before continuing uphill in the same direction over a moorland of streams and peat-cutting. After just over 1 mile of hard going, you will find yourself approaching the western edge of the plateau where further cliffs overlook a series of small lakes nestling in the aptly named Coumalocha (corrie of the lakes).

Here turn right and you will have plenty of opportunities to admire the fine views from this side of the mountain as you proceed northward along the edge of the plateau, until you come to the next of the corries. This one has two lakes, the Sgilloges, and beyond it can be seen the bridle path passing up through The Gap backed by the spectacular Knockanaffrin ridge. Turn right along the edge of the corrie, and after crossing the streams which fall into it, continue uphill to the east across an area of deep, pebble-filled peat hags. After little over 1 mile of this rather featureless landscape, you should be approaching the edge of Coumshingaun again, so proceed cautiously if visibility is bad. When you reach the cliffs skirt round them to the left until you arrive at the well-grassed cone of Staicin-min (2,308 ft, smooth peak). Carry on now along the ridge which confronts you, past the rocks which dominate its eastern end, and then descend cautiously to the right at the end of the ridge so as to regain the lake close to its outlet.

For the full walk which covers, about 10 miles and 3,000 ft of ascent, you should allow at least 5 hours excluding halts, and bear in mind that, should the weather be bad, intelligent use of map and compass will be extremely important.

Map: ½″ sheet 22.

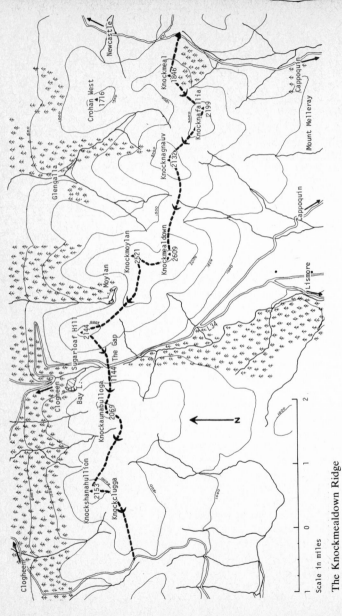

The Knockmealdown Ridge

Scale in miles

Clogheen

Knockshanahullion
2153

Knockcurragh

Knockaunabulloga
2069

Bay L.

Clogheen

Sugarloaf Hill
1344

1144 The Gap

F.134

Lismore

Moylan

Knockmoylan
2521

Knockmealdown
2609

Knockagnauv
2132

Knocknafallia
2199

Knockmeal
1846

Crohan West
1716

Glengalla

Newcastle

Cappoquin

Mount Melleray

Cappoquin

N

9 The Knockmealdown Ridge

Take the Cappoquin turning off the Dungarvan–Lismore road
(N72) and follow the Newcastle road north past Mount Melleray to
its highest point, before parking close to a rusted gate on the left (MR
111081).

A ditch heading uphill to the west, which also defines the county
boundary, marks your route and this should be followed to its
junction with another ditch close to the summit of Knockmeal
(1,846 ft, bare hill). Take the left-hand fork and follow it downhill
until you arrive at the corner of a forestry plantation. The ditch here
turns right, but you should leave it and continue south up the steep
hillside to arrive at the large cairn marking the summit of
Knocknafallia (2,199 ft, hill of the walls) which has good views over
the distinctive grey buildings of Mt Melleray. Now turn right and
cross a shallow saddle, before rejoining the ditch close to the
summit of Knocknagnauv (2,132 ft, hill of the bones), a flattish
peak of little distinction, overlooking Glengalla. From here the
route follows the ditch which first swings left – or south-west – and
then turns to the west before dropping sharply into the valley which
divides the eastern Knockmealdowns. After crossing the track
running through this valley – now becoming rather difficult to see –
a stiff climb up the steep eastern slope of Knockmealdown (2,609 ft,
bare brown mountain) ensues. At the summit of this fine peak,
which is marked only by a trig-point, rest for a while to appreciate
the lovely view southwards over Lismore and Cappoquin where the
River Blackwater makes its sweep towards the sea. Near at hand to
the north, across the head of the Glengalla valley, is Knockmoylan
and beyond it can be seen the long high Galty ridge, whilst the
Comeraghs dominate the view to the east.

From Knockmealdown stay close to the ditch until it turns left,
where a short detour can be made to the north-east to visit the
summit rocks of Knockmoylan (2,521 ft). Back at the ditch (plate
17) there is a gentle descent into a col overlooking the valley of
Lough Moylan on the right and the usually busy motor road
between Lismore and Clogheen on the left; and then a short climb
brings you to the cairns at the summit of Sugarloaf (2,144 ft). This is
a superb viewpoint, particularly looking north over the fertile

17 Following the ditch from Knockmealdown towards the Sugarloaf, with the Galty ridge in the background

18 The Knockmealdowns, from the north

Mitchelstown plain. Below can be seen one of the country's finest mountain roads over The Gap.

Close to the Sugarloaf, the ditch durns sharply left and it should now be followed down the steep hillside to arrive at the highest point of the metalled road. This is a handy spot to end the walk, but those who wish to complete the full range will continue following the ditch up the opposite side of the pass. At the top of the slope, where the ditch forks, the required route is to the west, to the summit of Knockaunabulloga (2,069 ft). From there you should bear first left and then swing right around the head of a wide valley. Around here there are further traces of an indistinct ditch, but as the ground begins to rise again you should leave the ditch and head north-west until you reach the large stone pile distinguishing the summit of Knockshanahullion (2,153 ft, hill of the old elbow). The final section of the walk is to the south-west, first across a shallow saddle to the cairn at Knockclugga, and then following a turf-cutters' path down to the metalled road which crosses the range here and which can be used as a convenient finishing point.

This road in fact connects with the L28 about ½ mile west of Clogheen, and is a useful means of access, for none of the other roads shown on the OS map around this area is extant.

The going in the Knockmealdowns (plate 18) is often excellent, and never less than good. The full walk of 12 miles and 4,400 ft of ascent should take about 6¼ hours, while the section to The Gap would take 4 hours (both of these times are exclusive of halts). You will notice, however, that for both walks you must either have a car to meet you at the end, or walk all the way back to the start.

Map: ½" sheet 22.

10 Galty Mountains main ridge

The traverse of the main ridge at the western end of the Galty mountains is a superb grassy walk, maintaining a height of over 2,500 ft for most of its length. The relative isolation of this range makes for fine aspects in all directions, the view down the steep northern slopes into the Glen of Aherlow being particularly impressive.

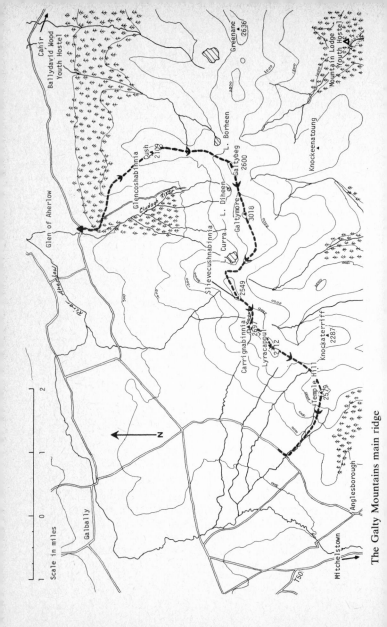

The Galty Mountains main ridge

19 The north side of the Galty ridge from Ballinacourty. Cush is in the centre and Galtymore on the right

From Cahir drive along the minor road which skirts the northern side of the mountains (plate 19) and park close to the bridge at the end of Glencoshabinnia (MR 871280). (Ballydavid Wood Youth Hostel is also on this road.) Turn up the boreen on the eastern side of the bridge (not shown on the map) and stay on it until you reach the edge of the forest. Then turn left and follow the fence for less than 1 mile. Now bear right and climb uphill by a faint ditch until the angle of ascent steepens and you reach the low crags at the summit of Cush (2,109 ft, *Cos*, foot) from where you have a fine view over the enclosed valleys of Glencush and Rossbog.

From Cush the route is almost due south, dropping sharply into a marshy col and then climbing past the west side of Lough Borheen (plate 20) which was once approached by a mountain road. The pull up to Galtybeg (2,600 ft), keeping to the right of the cliffs behind the lake, is a hard one, but there is little shelter to be had at the summit and if the weather is bad you will not linger and rest but hurry down its western ridge into an area of deep peat-hags close to the great cliffs overlooking Lough Diheen (vat or tub). From here another hard slog takes you past springs (from which you can drink even in the driest weather) and soon the eastern end of the long summit plateau of Galtymore (3,018 ft, *Sliabh na gCoillteadh*, wooded mountain) is reached. This is Ireland's highest inland mountain, and there are superb views in every direction with Lough Derg and the Shannon shining to the north-west and the sea sometimes visible far to the south. A history of crosses being placed here has been maintained, for although the stone ones erected in 1932 and 1953 have both been victims of the weather, a metal

20 Lough Borheen, with Galtybeg behind it

21 The western end of the Galty ridge from the north, looking across the Glen of Aherlow: Galtymore (left), Slievecushnabinnia (centre), Carrignabinnia, Lyracappul and Temple Hill (right)

Celtic cross was put up by local people in 1975.

A short descent to the west will now take you to a flat, rather desolate area and the route then swings to the right and follows a stone wall which begins here. The wall passes close to the steep cliffs above Lough Curra and then climbs gently until it turns sharply left close to the cairn marking the summit of Slievecushnabinnia, (2,549 ft, mountain at the foot of the peak – Galtymore is the peak). Continue by the wall across a rather wet area with good views into the southern valleys, and near to a slight bend you will see the cairn of Carrignabinnia (2,697 ft) on your right. You will now be passing close to the northern escarpment from which the ground falls away steeply into the Glen of Aherlow, and if the weather is fine the stretch up to Lyracappul (2,712 ft) is superb ridge-walking (plate 21). The wall ends close to that summit and you should now turn to the south-west, descending through old peat-cuttings and then crossing the head of the valley before commencing the final climb up to the enormous mound of stones at the summit of Temple Hill (2,579 ft).

Just below Temple Hill, and to the west of it, is a rocky spur which guides your way down. From it there is a small path which can be followed to the edge of a forestry plantation, and you should then bear right across the fields towards the farm buildings which lie close to the metalled road.

The distance covered is about 11 miles with roughly 4,000 ft of climbing, but the underfoot conditions are usually very good and a reasonably fit walker will complete the traverse in less than 6 hours, excluding halts.

Note: From Mountain Lodge Youth Hostel you can do this same walk by following the forest tracks until it is possible to break out to the west to reach the track which goes over Knockeenatoung nearly to the summit of Galtybeg.

Maps: ½″ sheets 18 and 22.

11 Keeper Hill and Silvermine Mountain

Keeper Hill (plate 22) presents little challenge from the climbing point of view, but is the highest peak in the North Tipperary area and as such has good views over the many lower rounded hills which are a feature of this part of the country.

Leave the T19 at Newport, and follow the minor road north-east, until, just before Crishanagh you turn right on to a road which follows the Mulkear River. After about 1 mile you will pass a new bungalow on the right, immediately beyond which there is a narrow surfaced boreen heading down towards the river. Park conveniently close to the junction (MR 798688) and follow the boreen over the bridge and on until you reach a forested hillside. Take the left-hand track which will lead you to the corner of the wood. Before you now can be seen the attractive corrie of Coumaniller and it is as well to start making height here up the grassy hillside so as to reach the

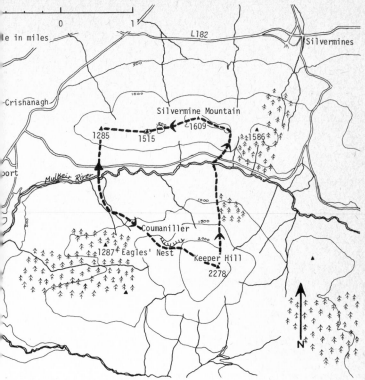

Keeper Hill and Silvermine Mountain

corrie at its upper western edge. The route then follows the rim of the corrie past the crags at the Eagles' Nest to where a couple of low stone cairns stand above possible megalithic remains.

Here bear slightly right and make your way across the gently sloping plateau until you reach the cairned summit of Keeper Hill (2,279 ft). To the north-west, the upper and lower reaches of Lough Derg attract the eye on both sides of the Arra Mountains, whilst to the south Mother Mountain is the most distinctive of the nearer

22 Keeper Hill, from the north-west

23 The Silvermine ridge from the north-west

hills. Beyond them the Galtees dominate the far skyline, with
Slievenamon and the Comeraghs also prominent further east.
Keeper Hill and its environs attained prominence in Irish history in
1690, for Patrick Sarsfield camped here before his attack on the
Williamite siege-train in Limerick. Ninety years before that they
were crossed by the forces of O'Neill and O'Donnell on their way to
the Battle of Kinsale.

The route from the summit is to the north past the edge of a small
corrie, and you then descend a fairly rough hillside by keeping to
the left of a forestry plantation. At the foot of the slope bear slightly
left and head across the fields towards a farm standing in a copse of
trees on the far side of the river. Adjacent to the farm is a narrow
wooden footbridge – the only dry river crossing hereabouts –
beyond which a sandy lane winds up to the motor road above. You
can now turn left and follow this road back to your starting point,
but a more interesting alternative offers itself in the shape of the
Silvermine ridge (plate 23). Reach this by crossing the metalled
road, avoiding some unfriendly furze bushes at the foot of the slope,
and climbing due north up the left-hand side of a narrow valley until
you reach the ditch at the top.

Now turn left and climb slightly to the 1,609-ft hill which is the
highest point of the ridge and which overlooks the mines on the
northern slopes. The mine buildings, settling ponds, and waste
dumps do nothing to enhance the view, but the fact that these
operations have been carried out here for nearly 700 years is
indicative of their importance to the area. The route continues west
along the edge of the low escarpment until the end of the ridge is
reached. Then bear left and pick the best way down through the
fields to reach the road close to the junction.

The going is generally quite easy, with less than 3,000 ft of
climbing, and the 7-mile walk should be comfortably accomplished
in 4 hours, excluding halts.

Map: $\frac{1}{2}''$ sheet 18.

Kerry and Cork sandstone

The same east-west Armorican folding which created the mountains of the South-east has, in the South-west, produced a series of parallel folds which form the finest concentration of mountains in Ireland. The sea has flooded the troughs of the folds, leaving gnarled and knobbly fingers projecting into the Atlantic.

The most northerly finger forms the long, narrow Dingle Peninsula, culminating in Mount Brandon, which at least one Scotsman has claimed is the finest mountain in the British Isles. The second finger, the Iveragh Peninsula, broad and stubby, contains Carrauntoohil and all but three of the 3,000-ft mountains of Ireland. The mountains of the third finger, the Beara Peninsula, though lower, are still interesting, but the other fingers, south of Bantry Bay, although they contain much rough country, have no hills high enough to claim our attention.

The Kerry and Cork mountains are all sandstone, and because of the temperate oceanic climate, they carry much vegetation. The typical mountain of the region is quite steep, with outcrops of purple rock projecting through the dark green-brown vegetation. Gloomy corries with dark, wet cliffs are common. The ridges vary; sometimes, as in the Macgillycuddy's Reeks, they form true arêtes; more often, as on Brandon, they will have one steep and one gentle slope; or, as in the Beara Peninsula, the ridges may be broad and level, but edged with cliffs.

The mountains round Killarney in the Iveragh Peninsula are, probably deservedly, the most popular ones in the area, but the rest of the region should not be neglected. Brandon is in a class by itself, the mountains at the western end of the Iveragh Peninsula are rough, wild, and unfrequented, and in addition to the walks listed on the Beara Peninsula, the long ridge walk from Allihies to Gougane Barra is a magnificent expedition.

Train and bus services
For general access the area is well served by public transport. There

are trains from Dublin, Limerick, and Cork, three times daily, via Killarney to Tralee; and buses from Cork to Glengarriff daily (for the Beara Peninsula), to Killarney daily (for the Iveragh Peninsula), and to Tralee several times a week (for the Dingle Peninsula). In summer there is also a daily service from Cork via Glengarriff and Kenmare over Moll's Gap to Killarney, with a connection to Tralee.

In the Dingle Peninsula there are daily buses from Tralee to Dingle (passing the start of Route 19, and not far from Conair Pass, Route 18) while branch services (infrequent!) to Castle Gregory and Ballydavid leave you just about within reach of Brandon by Route 18A.

In the Iveragh Peninsula there is a daily bus from Killarney through Killorglin to Cahirciveen, giving access to Routes 14 and 16 with a long walk, and directly to the start of Route 17.

For the Beara Peninsula (in addition to the Cork-Glengarriff service already mentioned) there is a daily bus from Killarney to Kenmare, but there are no buses further west.

Car access
The N22 (Cork-Killarney-Tralee) and the N21/23 (Limerick-Killarney) are the main access roads to the area. The Dingle Peninsula has coast roads north and south for most of its length, and several roads across its width, one serving Route 19, and the other, Conair Pass, serving Route 18. The N70 (Ring of Kerry) goes right around the Iveragh Peninsula, but except for Route 17, it does not open up any good walks. The network of roads around the Macgillycuddy's Reeks make access to Route 12–15 easy, but do not try to drive through the Gap of Dunloe in high summer, you will risk the active displeasure of pony-hirers! Instead, you should explore the two high passes out of Glencar, the Ballaghbeama to the south (Route 16) and the Ballaghadereen to the west towards Waterville. The latter offers fine views of the Reeks, and provides access to Knocknagantee and Coomcallee, a fine area of rough hills which almost deserved a route in this guide. The N71 south from Killarney takes you towards Mangerton (Route 12), over Moll's Gap (fine views both north and south) down to Kenmare, and through the heart of the Caha Mountains to Glengarriff. The coast

roads round the Beara Peninsula (L62, north, and L61, south), and
the scenic mountain road over the Healy Pass, provide access to
Routes 20 and 21.

Accommodation
The Beara and Iveragh Peninsulas are well supplied with youth
hostels, almost enough to make continuous touring possible on foot.
From Loo Bridge Hostel near the N22 in the east, Mangerton
(Route 12) is just possible. Aghadoe (Killarney) is well-placed for
Route 13 and not impossible for Route 12. Routes 14 and 15 are
well served by the Corran tuathail Hostel at the entrance to the
Hag's Glen on the north, and the Black Valley Hostel on the south.
There are no An Óige hostels further west but there are two private
bunkhouses (details from FMCI) in Glencar – the Climbers' Inn (MR
725841) and the Mountain Hut (MR 773816). In the Beara
Peninsula Allihies Hostel is too far west to be useful, but the
Glanmore Lake Hostel is ideal for Routes 20 and 21, and there is
also a good walk along the ridge over Knockowen to the next hostel
at Bonane on the Kenmare-Glengarriff section of the N71. (From
Bonane, there is a good horseshoe walk over Knockboy, which only
just missed inclusion in our 50 routes).
  Cork and Kerry is a tourist region, so there is no lack of hotels,
farmhouses, and 'B and Bs', but we would advise you to avoid the
main tourist centres, which are crowded and generally expensive.
As elsewhere, camping is generally possible with the landowner's
permission.

Maps
The 1″ Killarney District is most useful, covering not only the
Reeks, but also the best part of the Beara Peninsula. There is also a
small special 1″ map of Brandon (published for the Leaving
Certificate Examination a few years ago) which may still be
available from the OS office in Dublin. The area is covered by three
½″ maps, sheet 20 for the Dingle and Iveragh Peninsulas, sheet 21
for the mountains east of the line Killorglin to Kenmare, and sheet
24 for the Beara Peninsula.

12 **Mangerton** (Iveragh Peninsula)

Killarney is internationally renowned for its beauty. It is a pity (or is
it?) that the majority of travellers to the area confine themselves to
the lower ground, the path to the top of Torc Waterfall being the
height of their ambition. The panoramic views given from the
summit of Mangerton (perhaps *Mong phortach*, the long-grassed
bog, plate 24) are seldom seen.

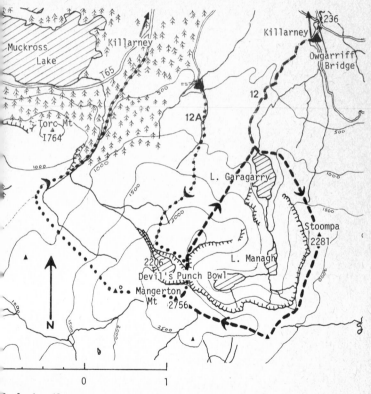

Mangerton

24 Evening clouds on Mangerton, from across Lough Leane

The circuit of Glenacappul (horses' glen) is the most ambitious way of gaining the summit, and there are a number of alternative routes, some little more than gentle walks. However, a warning note must be struck: the higher ground here boasts the heaviest rainfall in Ireland, fog and mist are regular features, and the broad indefinite expanse of the summit calls for navigating ability to avoid an unforeseen descent over sheer coum walls.

The Glenacappul horseshoe (Route 12) is most easily begun at Coolies, where a bridge (MR 005855) gives access to a pair of gates. The unsurfaced road through the left gate leads to a path which travels uphill on the west side of the Owgarriff river. A wooden bridge crosses it at the outlet of Lough Garagarry, and you can now zigzag up the heather-clad shoulder to the double summit of Stoompa (2,281 ft, the higher one). The rocky summits give way to the peat banks of the saddle to the south, from where you travel ssw above the walls of the magnificent coum. Glenacappul is a perfect

25 The Devil's Punch Bowl

example of the paternoster-lake-dotted valley scoured out by ice. The floor of the valley is rough – otherwise, I would recommend a route through it. It is possible to ascend through the south-west wall above Lough Erhogh but extreme care is called for. Assuming you are still above, looking down, continue more or less west to the ill-defined summit of Mangerton (2,756 ft). The expansive top consists of a multiplicity of high peat banks, eroded in places to reveal the gravel beneath. The actual summit is marked with a cairn which has a simple upright stone at the centre.

From the summit, travel north to the arête between Glenacappul and the Devil's Punch Bowl (plate 25). This is a good place to pause to admire the carving of the Ice Ages, examples of which are to left and right. On a windy day it may not be comfortable, of course. If your car has been left at Coolies, continue north over the unnamed peak and descend to Lough Garagarry to follow the path by which you entered.

This walk is 9½ miles with 3,400 ft of ascent, and will take you about 5 hours, exclusive of halts.

For a shorter walk to the Devil's Punch Bowl (Route 12A), take the Kenmare road, and leave it by the first turn east after the Muckross Hotel, signposted *Mangerton Viewing Park*. Pass the park and walk as far as the concrete bridge at the end of the surfaced road. From here a former bridle path runs more or less south all the way to the Bachelor's Well at the outlet of the Devil's Punch Bowl. A circuit of the Punch Bowl can be extended to include Mangerton Summit. Unless you feel obliged to return by the bridle path, you can descend west to the Torc (Owengarriff) River valley. The Queen's Drive shown on the maps as a somewhat undefined path has, in fact, been recently surfaced. It seems to us a great pity so to pander to the motorized traveller as to endanger further the deer which inhabit the slopes of Mangerton and Torc Mountains. Each incursion into the former wilderness pushes the deer back further.

The Naismith time for this walk (7 miles and 2,650 ft of ascent) is about 4 hours, excluding halts.

Maps: 1″ sheet Killarney District, ½″ sheets 20 or 21.

13 **Purple Mountain** (Iveragh Peninsula)

Between the Lakes of Killarney and the spectacular Gap of Dunloe lies the ridge composed of Tomies and Purple Mountains (plates 26 and 27), which is the basis of a fine day's walking. An outlier to the east, Shehy Mountain, is a good vantage point for viewing the Killarney Lakes.

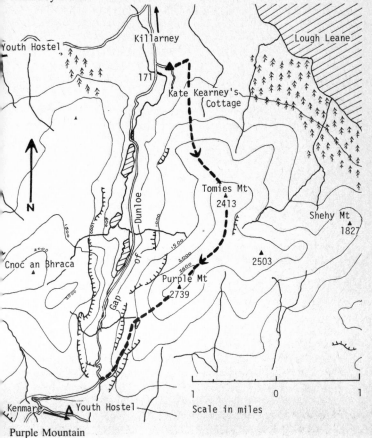

Purple Mountain

26 Morning light on Purple and Tomies Mts, from across Lough Leane

Park your car at Kate Kearney's Cottage at the entrance to the
Gap of Dunloe. Return north about ½-mile. After crossing the
bridge over the River Lee, take the unsurfaced road (MR 882892)
leading east through two gates to join the spur which runs roughly
south. Sheep tracks run each side of the fence, which initially
follows the spur. The ascent towards Purple is gentle, even if
deceptive for first-timers – the rounded nature of the slope
providing a series of false summits. However, the top of Tomies
(2,413 ft) will be recognized by the change to scree from what has
been a thick growth of heather. The stone mounds there are said to
be burial places.

During the ascent to Tomies, views will have been enlarging, with
the island-dotted Lower Lake (Lough Leane) on your left, and the
spire of Killarney Cathedral marking the town beyond. The Gap of
Dunloe is such a narrow cleft that it cannot be seen in its entirety
from this point. West beyond it is the jagged ridge of the
MacGillycuddy Reeks, and the zigzag path on the slope of Strickeen

Hill directly across is the start of the Reeks Walk. From Tomies, descend more or less directly south before ascending again to the 2,400-ft level. Here there is the option of travelling east over the 2,503-ft top (Shehy Mor) for views from Shehy. Otherwise, you continue south-west on the narrow peat ridge-top to the scree-clad summit of Purple Mountain (2,739 ft).

From the top of Purple, it is possible to descend south or south-east to the Upper Lake. However, I suggest you benefit from the views into Cummeenduff Glen by travelling ssw to Glas Lough and following the stream, to gain the road just south of the head of the Gap.

Your course then depends on your ultimate destination. If you have to return to your car, a walk north through the deep ice-carved gorge of the Gap of Dunloe will provide a very satisfying end to the day. If you are bound for the Black Valley Hostel, the map shows

27 View from Torc Mt – from right to left, Tomies Mt, Shehy Mor, Purple Mt and, behind, the Eastern Reeks

the path south from the road. If you intend returning to Killarney, you can also drop down to the hostel and then continue on the road east to the site of Lord Brandon's Cottage. There is a tea-house there, where you may wish to pause before following the path (marked on the 1" map) east through Derrynaheirka and Derrycunnihy. (This path is to be one of the stages of the Kerry Long-Distance Route.) Evening seems the ideal time to walk through the peace of the lakeside woods. The Kenmare road leads to Killarney town.

This walk (exclusive of any return route or the diversion to Shehy Mountain) is 6 miles long, with 2,900 ft of ascent, and will take at least 3½ hours, without halts.

Maps: 1" sheet Killarney District, ½" sheets 20 or 21.

14 Carrauntoohil (Iveragh Peninsula)

As Ireland's highest summit, one would expect Carrauntoohil (plate 28) to dominate its surroundings. This however, it does not do – simply because it is connected by ridges to the greatest concentration of 3,000-ft peaks in this island. As a result, the MacGillycuddy Reeks provide most magnificent climbing. The scenery is dramatic in the extreme, and route after route offers variations in climbing and views. Weather of course, will dictate whether you have those views: it is seldom that the summit lacks a cover of cloud or mist. May and September are said to be the best months, although the annual climb on 26 December seems as often as any to provide good visibility.

The conventional approach to Carrauntoohil is from the north through Coomcallee (Hag's Glen) (plate 29). This has the advantage of presenting an uninterrupted view of the north-east face, a perfect conical shape resembling everyone's impression of what a mountain should be and offering encouragement to make the necessary effort. A route from the south through Cummeenduff Glen (Black Valley) joins it at the top of the col (scarcely a saddle) at the 2,200-ft level, before the scree slope ascent north-east to the summit. A horseshoe ridge-walk begins and ends near Lough Acoose to the west. This offers more testing conditions across the

28 Carrauntoohil, from Caragh Lake

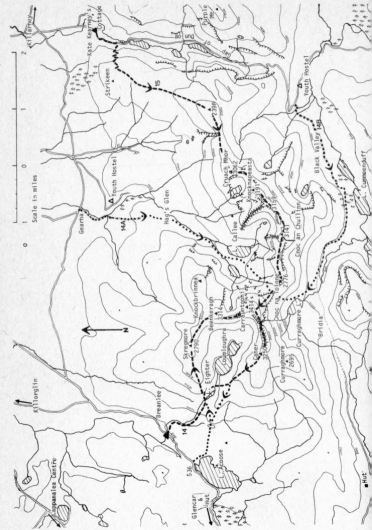

Carrauntoohil and the Eastern Reeks

arête joining Beenkeragh to Carrauntoohil. The ultimate is, of course, the MacGillycuddy Reeks Ridge climb, an 11-mile trek from the Gap of Dunloe (in the east) to Lough Acoose (in the west) over six peaks above the 3,000-ft level. There is an annual 'walk' along this route on the Sunday of the May/June holiday weekend. Other routes, such a a circuit of Coomcallee or the ascent through Cummeenoughter (Eagles' Nest on the OS map) will suggest themselves to the enthusiast.

Of the shorter routes, the best is probably the Coumloughra horseshoe (Route 14). This includes the three highest summits, and as already noted, there is a narrow difficult ridge between Beenkeragh (3,314 ft, *Beann caorach*, the peak of the sheep) and Carrauntoohil (3,414 ft, *Corran tuathail* – Tuathail is probably the name of a person or tribe). The start can be from Lough Acoose (MR 766859) where the annual walk ends, or beside the bridge at Breanlee (MR 767867). Cross the stream to the west of Lough

29 Caher (left), Carrauntoohil (centre) and Beenkeragh (right), from Knocknapeasta. In the foreground are Loughs Callee and Gouragh

30 Caher from the summit of Carrauntoohil

Eighter and ascend to the rocky top of Skregmore (2,790 ft, *Screag mhor*, the large rough hill). Continue along the ridge over the 2,750-ft top and up the rocky shoulder to Beenkeragh. From the summit, provided you have visibility, the nature of the route ahead is clear. Care should obviously be taken crossing the arête. There seems to be an advantage in not remaining on the top but seeking sheep tracks which run some feet below. There is a steeper ascent to the summit of Carrauntoohil, which is marked by a large steel cross erected in 1977. If you are lucky enough to have a clear day, you can look back along the knife-edge towards Beenkeragh, and then north and east to the astonishing Devil's Looking-glass Lake, surrounded on three sides by crags, and further away the big lakes of the Hag's Glen. For the descent, retrace your steps for a little, and then swing first south-west and then west towards Caher (3,250 ft, *Cathair*, the fort, plate 30). Do not be discouraged by the number of rises; Caher has three summits, of which the middle is the highest. From Caher go north-west (take care not to drift south to

Curraghmore) either to rejoin the stream at Lough Eighter and continue down to Breanlee, or to strike west to Lough Acoose.

An easier alternative (Route 14A) starts from Gearha (MR 830892) on the upper road from Glencar to the Gap of Dunloe. Go up the road beside the Gaddagh river, and park your car beside the bridge over the Glasheencorgoad stream. Follow the green road (forking left at the Y-junction) past Lisleibane into the Hag's Glen. You can also reach this point from the nearby youth hostel, but it may be difficult to cross the river. The green road continues in the glen, to cross at the ford (1,080 ft). Continue south at that stage through peat bog between Lough Gouragh and Lough Callee. The esk (gully) named the Devil's Ladder is obvious straight ahead. Following the traditional route up the Ladder, you arrive at a boggy crest giving views into Cummeenduff and the Bridia Valley. There is approximately another 1,200 ft up the rough scree-covered slope to the summit. While there are cairns at intervals, these do not stand out in the mass of loose rock. The rise is eased somewhat by keeping a course more to the west to meet the ridge joining Caher to Carrauntoohil. There is a choice of routes in descent: you can take either of the arms of the Coumloughra horseshoe; or you can return to the top of the Devil's Ladder, and either go back down the Hag's Glen, or descend to the Black Valley. If you go back to the top of the Ladder, take care to follow the cairned route if there is mist, as there are many crags inadequately marked on the map.

Another route (Route 14B) starts from the Black Valley Youth Hostel (MR 865827). Follow the surfaced road to the south of Cummeenduff Lough. Continue on the unsurfaced road, which is now to the north of the Cummeenduff River, to reach the last houses in the glen. A path leads from there into the Bridia Valley, but this can be left at a suitable point to gain Curraghmore Lake. From the western end of the lake, an obvious grassy gully leads to the col above the Devil's Ladder from where the ascent can be made as already described.

The Coumloughra horseshoe (Route 14) is 8 miles long, with 3,800 ft of ascent, and will take at least 4½ hours, excluding halts.

Route 14A, the Hag's Glen route (returning the same way) is 7 miles long, with 3,000 ft of ascent, and should take 4 hours without halts.

Route 14B (returning the same way) is 11 miles long, with 3,200 ft of ascent, and will take nearly 5½ hours, excluding halts.

Maps: 1" sheet Killarney District, ½" sheets 20 or 21.

15 The Eastern Reeks (Iveragh Peninsula) *See map on p 104*

To the east of the Devil's Ladder a long line of rocky peaks, several of them more than 3,000 ft in height, stretches away to the Gap of Dunloe (plate 31). The route of the Reeks Walk follows this ridge from Kate Kearney's Cottage in the Gap of Dunloe, over the Eastern Reeks to the top of the Ladder, up to Carrauntoohil and descends to Lough Acoose over Caher. It is a demanding walk, and unless you are fit, and the weather is good, you may prefer to take it in two bites. The first section is described below (the second section is described under Route 14, Carrauntoohil).

From Kate Kearney's Cottage (MR 882887) at the entrance to the Gap of Dunloe follow the unsurfaced road south until a green road zigzagging towards the summit of Strickeen Hill is seen. Follow this in its ascent, and also as it turns south-west (avoiding the top of Strickeen). Continue to the top of Cnoc an Bhraca (2,398 ft). The scree-covered slope gives some impression of what is ahead, but it is not until one has descended to the col over Alohart and begun the ascent towards Cruach Mhor that the true nature of the Reeks is seen. The slope ahead is completely covered with scree (perhaps better described as massive shattered boulders) and the jagged character of the arête leading south from Cruach Mhor is obvious.

At the summit of Cruach Mhor (3,162 ft, large stack) is a tiny grotto (now lacking a statue). The journey along the arête is eased by moving down, right, on the first leg towards Lough Cummeennapesta until the unnamed peak (3,100 ft) is reached. The arête leading west is not as dangerous, but again can be avoided by taking sheep tracks on the left side. An easy ascent leads to the summit of Knocknapeasta (3,191 ft, hill of the serpent, plate 32). This is a good point to relax before continuing on the rest of the walk. The journey wsw over Bearna Rua (3,159 ft, not on maps) and on to Cnoc an Chuilinn (3,141 ft, hill of the holly tree) is across a broad peat bog, as is the ridge over Cnoc na Toinne (2,776 ft). A

31 The Eastern Reeks ridge from the Hag's Glen. Cruach Mhor is on the left, and the Devil's Ladder is the depression in the ridge on the extreme right

32 The Knocknapeasta ridge, looking east towards the Killarney lakes

short descent brings you to the col over the Devil's Ladder. From the top of the Ladder, follow the ridge to Carrauntoohil or else descend either to the Hag's Glen or Black Valley (see Route 14).

The length of the walk from Kate Kearney's Cottage to the road at Gearha is 11 miles, with 4,200 ft of ascent; you should allow at least 6 hours, exclusive of halts.

The actual Reeks Walk is 11 miles, with 6,000 ft of ascent – a good 7 hours without halts. It is same length as the Hag's Glen route, but there is a lot more climbing – and at the end of the day!

Maps: 1″ sheet Killarney District, ½″ sheets 20 or 21.

16 **Mullaghanattin** (Iveragh Peninsula)

Glencar has in recent years become a major centre for adventure sports. The MacGillycuddy Reeks are within easy reach, and the conical shape of Mullaghanattin (2,539 ft, summit of the gorse) lures the keen walker – a circuit of the Cloon Lakes gives a good day's outing. I should emphasize that the latter is a full day's journey, and attempting it other than in summer will almost certainly lead to your being benighted.

If you have a companion who can collect you at the end of the day or drive your car to the finishing point for you, the conventional starting point for Mullaghanattin (plate 33) is near the top of the Ballaghbeama Pass (852 ft, MR 756781). There is a scramble through rock faces to the top of Knockavulloge (1,505 ft) from where the ascent to the summit of Mullaghanattin is more gentle. If the day is clear, much of south Kerry is visible from here.

A ridge now runs south-west. At first this is grassy, enticing you to bound along over the summit of Beoun (2,468 ft *Beann*, peak). Later, the true nature of the Cloon Circuit becomes clear. The grass ridge changes to rock seams with a multiplicity of minor ascents and descents. While it is not necessary to take in Finnararagh (2,185 ft), it is best to go close to it to avoid any danger of ending up amongst the sheer walls which mark the end of the Cloon Valley south of Lough Reagh (plate 34). Rock walls there are aplenty, and this is one of the areas in Kerry where rock climbs were first logged.

From the slopes of Finnararagh, set a course to take you down to

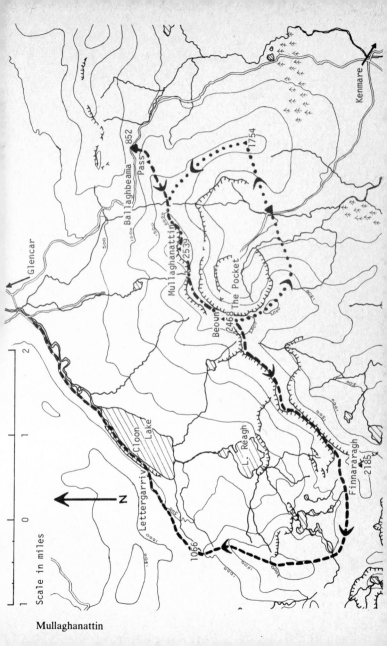

Mullaghanattin

Scale in miles

N

Glencar

Lettergarriv Cloon Lake

Ballaghbeama Pass 852

Mullaghanattin 2539

Beoun 2468

The Pocket

1754

Kenmare

L. Reagh

Finnararagh 2185

1066

33 Mullaghanattin and Beoun from the north

the west of the lakes above the south-west walls at the
1,400–1,500-ft level. There is no advantage in trying to descend
here. Even if you can find a route, you end up with a rough journey
across the floor of the Cloon Valley. It is best to ascend north-west
to the 2,000-ft level and then travel north to Ballytrusk (1,066 ft)
and descend to the houses at Lettergarriv. A car may not be driven
the entire distance, but can be met along the unsurfaced road which
runs west of Cloon Lake. This route is 9 miles long, and includes
3,400 ft of ascent. It is hard going, so you should allow 5½ hours,
exclusive of stops.

For shorter days there is the circuit of The Pocket. Some 4 miles
east of Ballaghbeama towards Sneem, there is a surfaced road
which travels wnw into Tooreenahone. Park at the end of the road

34 Lough Reagh, and the rocky wilderness north of Finnararagh

(MR 746756) – don't obstruct others – and take the line of choice around the horseshoe. A direct assault on the south face of Mullaghanattin provides a tedious climb, and I suggest a course ENE to Pt 1,754 ft, from where a gradual ascent leads to Mullaghanattin. An anti-clockwise route will give views of the Reeks, across Glencar to Dingle Bay early in the day, and of Kenmare Bay as you begin the homeward ssw leg. Take customary care in the sharpish descent. The walk is 5½ miles long with 2,700 ft of ascent, and you should allow 3¼ hours, exclusive of halts.

Map: 1″ sheet Killarney District for Mullaghanattin and ½″ sheet 20 for the rest.

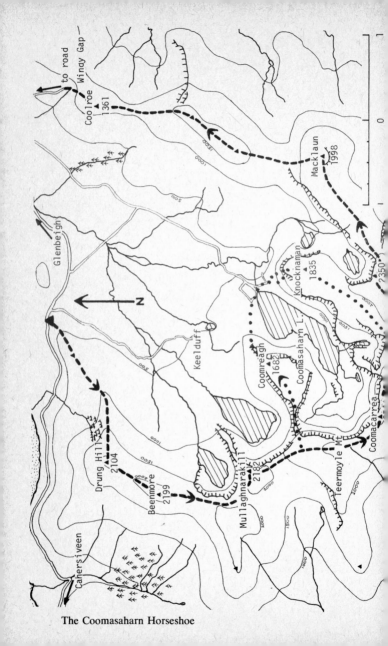

The Coomasaharn Horseshoe

17 The Coomasaharn Horseshoe (Iveragh Peninsula)

South and south-west of Glenbeigh village is the coum-dotted
Coomasaharn Range, which offers great choice of routes. Even the
shortest circuit gives a satisfying walk and dramatic views of land
and sea.

The main Horseshoe walk (plate 35) starts at Mountain Stage (MR
623888) about 4 miles west of Glenbeigh, where the spur leading
wsw to the top of Drung Hill (2,104 ft) is obvious. The gentle
ascent to Drung, and ssw to Beenmore, gives fine views of Dingle
Bay with the lonely Blasket Islands marking the nearest point to
America. The ridge continues south of Coomnacronia to
Mullaghnarakill (2,182 ft). If the day has been warm and you have
delayed, there is an escape route here north-east to Kealduff. Take

35 The Coomasaharn Horseshoe, from Coolroe Hill: left to right, Coomasaharn,
Coomaglasan and Coomnacronia

36 Coomreagh from the north-east

care in the steep descent. The south-east side of the sharp shoulder
is for rock-climbers only. The north-west side is less hazardous.

If determined to continue on the major Horseshoe, your route is
now more or less SSE to contour line 2,500 ft which lies east of
Teermoyle Mountain. The line on to Coomacarrea (2,541 ft) is
marked by an old boundary and this continues east to the point
south of Coomacullen which marks a further escape route, over
Knocknaman (*Cnoc na mBan*, peak of the women) to the
north-east. If using this descent, take care through the rock terraces
north of the 1,835-ft top.

The main Horseshoe continues over the grassy and flat summit of
Meenteog (2,350 ft) and then east of the final coum,
Coomeeneragh, to Macklaun (1,998 ft) and onwards north to
Beenreagh. Travelling now is heavier, with soft peat, long-grassed

and heathery, underfoot. Rather than continue over Seefin and
Commaun, you may decide to follow the old road which crosses the
Windy Gap just north of Coolroe Hill (1,361 ft) and takes you on a
northerly course down the High Road into Glenbeigh village.

This route is only for the long days of summer. It is 13 miles long,
with 4,400 ft of ascent, and will take you about 7 hours, exclusive of
halts.

A shorter route – which still requires a long day, although we
have travelled it in deep snow – is around Coomasaharn Lake itself.
For the benefit of fishermen, the lake is signposted from Glenbeigh.
Park when the lake comes into view. I suggest a clockwise route.
Zigzag up through the rock terraces of Knocknaman and from there
up to the slopes of Meenteog to arrive south of Coomacullen. The
line west to Coomacarrea is marked by the signs of an old boundary
wall mentioned already, and from there a line of stakes and stones
leads up the turf banks on the slopes of the 2,500-ft rise east of
Teermoyle. From here, travel north to where the line in from
Coomreagh (1,682 ft) to the north-east can be seen. There is a
grassy slope down to the arête which leads to the peaty triangle of
Coomreagh (plate 36). A course north-east will lead to the gentle
shoulder sloping down to the houses below. Please take care of
fences, and close all gates. There have been complaints about
damage done and rubbish left by day-trippers – fishermen, one
supposes; mountaineers would never forget the Country Code!

This shorter route is 6 miles long, with 2,600 ft of ascent, and will
take about 3¾ hours without halts.

Map: ½″ sheet 20.

18 **Mount Brandon** (Dingle Peninsula)
Outside of the Reeks, Brandon (plate 37) is Ireland's highest
mountain and many would call it the finest as well. You must climb
nearly every foot of its 3,127 ft, for it rises directly from the sea.

It is named of course for St Brendan the Navigator, and an
oratory dedicated to him marks the summit. He is supposed to have
meditated here before setting out in a curragh for Greenland and
America. (A few years ago a crew led by Tim Severin re-enacted the

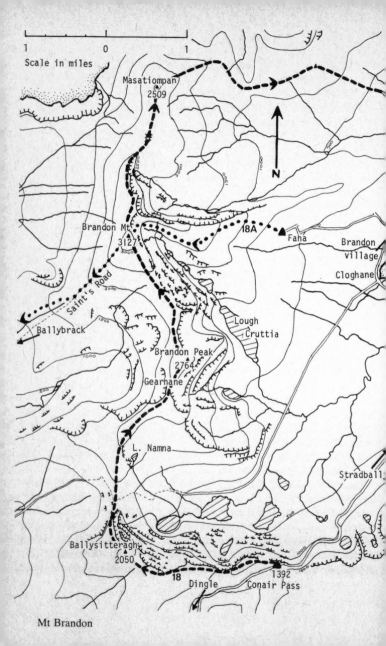

Scale in miles

1   0   1

Masatiompan
2509

N

Brandon Mt
3127

18A · · · Faha

Brandon
village

Cloghane

Saint's Road

Ballybrack

Lough
Cruttia

Brandon Peak
2764

Gearhane

L. Namna

Stradball

Ballysitteragh
2050

18
Dingle

1392
Conair Pass

Mt Brandon

37 The Brandon range from the east. The route from Faha (Route 18A) curls round the gentle cloud-dappled slopes just right of centre into the coum between these slopes and Brandon itself, which is the bold summit on the left

voyage, and reached Newfoundland safely in their curragh.)

The easiest way up Brandon is the Saint's Road from the west, but it is also the dullest, and the best approaches are from east or south. The ridge walk from Conair Pass is a perfect one in fine weather when one need not travel with too heavy a load. Underfoot, it is peat for almost the entire length, with a multiplicity of sheep tracks easing the way. Fell-running has recently been introduced to the country and it is easy to imagine this ridge could be a favourite course. However, its distance from any centre of population should preserve it for the lover of peace. As you walk, the sea is always ahead of you, and you seem almost to be on a promontory.

The route starts at the top of the Conair Pass (1,392 ft, MR 492056) with a gentle rise west to Ballysitteragh (2,050 ft). From there, circle north to the saddle. It is perhaps a little early to

38 A view down on the paternoster lakes to Lough Cruttia, with Ballysitteragh (right) and the Conair Pass (centre) in the background

mention an escape route but, if needed, the signs of a track running from Lough Gal (in the east) to Glin North (in the west) can be seen. This is said to have been a walking route in olden days from Cloghane to the hospital in Dingle.

A circuitous route now leads above Lough Namna by Gearhane to the summit of Brandon Peak (2,764 ft). From there one can bound along the gently sloping ridge to Brandon Mountain (3,127 ft) itself. Here are the remains of St Brendan's Oratory. A descent north about 300 ft leads to the path up the esk from the east, which is further described below.

The ridge walk continues on to Masatiompan (2,509 ft) from where you can choose your own route to Brandon village. If time remains you could visit the deserted village of Arraglen, or pause over the steep cliffs of Sauce Creek.

In recent years sheep fencing and gates have appeared on the eastern slopes of Masatiompan, and there have been stories of 'aggro' between determined motorcycle scramblers and sheep farmers who naturally wish to protect their flocks. Please maintain the good reputation of hill-walkers by using gates and not climbing over fences, and by closing all gates after use.

This route is 12 miles long, with 3,700 ft of ascent, and will take at least 6 hours without halts.

Although the ridge walk may give the 'top of the world' feeling, nothing can compare with the ascent of Mount Brandon through the eastern coum (Route 18A).

Start at Faha (MR 492119). The road to it is signposted from Cloghane village, and you begin near the grotto which marked the start of an annual pilgrimage. The warning posts (*Aire-Cnoc Gear*: Beware – Dangerous Mountain) were erected also to assist pilgrims, and they mark your route most of the way. The easily discerned path contours the east slope of the shoulder until you arrive at a well (marked Tobar) over Lough Nalacken. Here drama begins. The path now swings north-east through the coum with its walls of rippled rock, slopes of scree, and string of paternoster lakes (plate 38). To add to the spectacle, the coum contains many rare plants and flowers, which naturally, should never be picked.

At the inner end of the coum the path zigzags north-east up the

39 The summit of Mt Brandon from the north

esk to the north of Brandon itself. From the saddle it is a short rise of 300 ft or so to the summit (plate 39). You should, of course, be aware that almost sheer walls fall to the east of the path.

From the summit you can, if transport has been arranged, follow the route south-west of the Saint's Road. There is no obvious path leaving the top. Be careful that you do not wander into the coums and lakes on either side. The boggy expanse near the summit changes to a steeper rocky descent before you reach the wide stream bed which leads to Ballybrack.

Route 18A is a good bit shorter than the ridge walk – only about 5 miles, with 2,600 ft of ascent – but it is very rough and will take nearly 4 hours excluding halts.

You can, of course, make variations on these routes. Perhaps the best is to ascend from Faha and follow the ridge back to the Conair Pass. Another is to follow the chain of paternoster lakes all the way up from Lough Cruttia.

All these routes, as described, need a car at the point of descent, though you could make a round from Cloghane completely on foot.

Map: $\frac{1}{2}$" sheet 20. There is also a small coloured 1" map produced in 1972 for the Leaving Certificate Examination which is ideal if you can find a copy.

19 **Baurtregaum and Caherconree** (Dingle Peninsula)

An attraction of Corkaguiney (Dingle Peninsula) is the proximity of sea to the various summits (plate 40). Baurtregaum and Caherconree share common approaches and also share views of Tralee Bay to the north and Castlemaine Harbour to the south, as well as Dingle Bay and the Atlantic to the west.

From the north Derrymore Glen furnishes a very gradual and pleasant approach to both peaks. Three-quarters of a mile west of Derrymore School on the Dingle-Tralee road is a narrow hump-backed bridge (MR 743113). The (unsurfaced) road south beside it or the next (surfaced) road to the west will give access to the glen. A narrow gorge widens out and a route along the western side of the Derrymore River (not too close to the bank, which is rough) leads into the coum with its three paternoster lakes. Signs of former industrial use are to be seen along the route. These lakes were once used for the Derrymore Mill, the ruins of which stand near the main road. By the time you reach the third and highest lake, however, all signs of industry and commerce will be well behind you.

From the south-west corner of the coum there is a further gradual ascent to the saddle between Baurtregaum and Caherconree. It is a short 450-ft climb east to Baurtregaum (2,796 ft, summit of the three corries) or 350 ft west to the small cairn on Caherconree (2,713 ft, fort of Cu Roi Mac Daire).

But my preferred route to Caherconree takes one through the prehistoric fort of the same name. This route begins at Beheenagh (MR 715060) on the Bohernagloc road which runs from Camp village (in the north) to Aughils, on the Castlemaine-Inch road (in the south). The spine of the spur gives a natural ascent, with

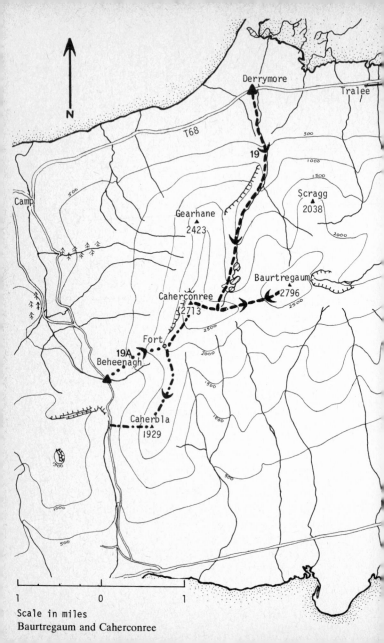

Scale in miles
Baurtregaum and Caherconree

40 Looking across Castlemaine Harbour to Baurtregaum (right) and Caherbla
(centre), with Caherconree in cloud behind

ever-enlarging views north and south until, just before reaching the
'gate' of the fort, Killarney Lower Lake can be seen to the east.
Before arriving at the fort, watch for the narrow openings of
underground channels which may be evidence of a geological fault.
The fort, on arrival at the 2,000-ft level, proves to be a natural rock
promontory on the north, west, and south sides which was enclosed
on the east by a stone wall in prehistoric times. Cu Roi Mac Daire,

the legendary creator of the fort, seems to have had magical powers far surpassing those of Merlin in the Arthurian legends.

A further 700-ft ascent past the rock stacks standing over the cliffs to the north – resist any temptation to climb the stacks, the rock can be fragile – attains Caherconree, and from there a traverse of 1 mile or so brings you to Baurtregaum. You could make a slight variation in descent by following the ridge ssw towards Caherbla (1,929 ft) and descending to road. This route is, in fact, marked with red and white poles. The true mountaineer frowns on such aids, as they encourage the 'high-heel shoes and handbag' brigade – I have seen them here! Only those adequately clothed to withstand the sudden changes in weather conditions which are a feature of our hills, and equipped with map and compass – which they are able to use – should take to the higher ground.

Naturally, if you have a second car you can make the complete north-south traverse.

The ascent of both summits from Derrymore, and return by the same route, is about 8 miles and 3,000 ft of ascent – say, about $4\frac{1}{2}$ hours without halts. Caherconree from Beheenagh, returning by Caherbla, is $4\frac{1}{2}$ miles and 2300 ft of ascent, and should take an easy 3 hours excluding stops.

Map: $\frac{1}{2}''$ sheet 20.

20 Hungry Hill (Beara Peninsula)

A feature of the hills of the south-west region, concentrated as they are on the three peninsulas of Beara, Iveragh and Dingle, is their proximity to the sea. The juxtaposition of water – whether sea, tarn, or corrie lake – with rock, heather slopes, and wild bogland provides an everchanging array of panoramic views and narrow vistas. The Beara Peninsula is on average only 9 miles wide, and deep ice-carved glens up to 6 miles long bring the sea inland, often almost meeting the coum lakes. Rock slabs and faces form sheer high walls, frequently showing the rippled layering of long-past geological activity.

This is the setting for Hungry Hill, which is the highest of the Caha Mountains and the highest in the Beara Peninsula. Its sheer

41 Hungry Hill from across Adrigole Harbour. The complete Coomgira circuit is visible

bulk, emphasized by its broad, almost plateau-like, top (plate 41), is most obvious travelling south-west on the road from Glengarriff to Adrigole. Coums eat into the east side, providing a very pleasant horseshoe circuit from Coomgira while a ridge approach from the NNE starting from the road at the top of Ballaghscart (now the Healy Pass), gives an easy gradual access. Both routes give views over a vast area, assuming that there is visibility; the Caha Mountains get their name from the Irish word *ceatha*, showers. Keep an eye on the weather.

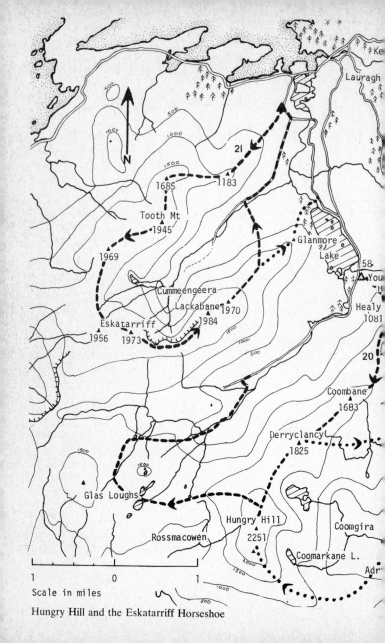

Hungry Hill and the Eskatarriff Horseshoe

Scale in miles

42 The Iveragh Mts from the top of the Healy Pass

Perhaps the best route is the circuit from Glanmore Youth Hostel (MR 780544). Immediately opposite the hostel a boreen leads up the hill through fields to the open hillside, which is climbed to the Healy Pass road, just north of the Pass. There is a fine view here north to the Iveragh Peninsula (plate 42). From the top of the Pass (Ballaghscart, 1,081 ft), the line of the walk is perfectly shown by the Cork-Kerry border. Leaving the slabs at Ballaghscart, travel across the boggy saddle to ascend to the more craggy summits of Coombane (1,683 ft) and Derryclancy (1,825 ft). Between these two is a lake which I believe is a year-round feature but which is not marked on the map. From Derryclancy descend to the saddle above Coomadayallig Lake, and climb gently over the north top to the summit of Hungry Hill (2,251 ft). It is worth the walk to continue to the south cairn from which there is a fine view south across Bantry Bay to the west Cork peninsula. In descent, from the south cairn keep west of the summit to join the ridge running to the Glas Loughs. This is rough going, with many little rocky ridges. A paint-marked route (made by Belgians who run a holiday centre near Lauragh) runs down fairly directly to the head of Glanmore above the last farm, but it is more interesting to go west past the Glas Loughs and keep along the county boundary to Clogher, before turning east to descend by the waterfalls to the valley. (The track shown on the OS map to the farm at MR 753516 is in fact a rough motor road.) There remains only a steady walk down the valley to the hostel.

This circuit is 10½ miles long with 2,400 ft of ascent, and will take nearly 5 hours, exclusive of halts.

Another pleasant route is the circuit of Coomgira. Just south of Adrigole village take the Bawn road which leads directly west into Coomgira. From the end of the road (MR 786493) there is an easy ascent to the shoulder to the south, from which you can travel north-west above the South Lake (Coomarkane Lake on the map) to reach the south cairn with its fine views to the south – and east for that matter, across Adrigole Harbour. Continue to the summit, and reverse the Glanmore route as far as Derryclancy, before swinging first east, and then south, to get back to your starting point.

This route is 5½ miles long with 1,900 ft of ascent – allow 3 hours without halts. (If you have left your car in Adrigole you could, of course, descend over Adrigole Mountain to the village.)

Map: 1″ Killarney District (You will need ½″ sheet 24 if you want to identify anything further south.)

21 **Eskatarriff Horseshoe** (Beara Peninsula) *See map on p 128*

Of the many coums which cut into the north side of the Beara Peninsula, my favourite is that of Cummeengeera, a short distance from a pleasant camping-spot at Lauragh. It is called The Pocket on the map, but the locals use this name for the head of the valley above Glanmore Lake (plate 43).

Follow the main road west from Lauragh School (MR 774583) towards Argroom for approximately ½-mile, and take the minor road leading south towards Glanmore Lake. Pass a shop and petrol station, and very shortly a path beside the next house on the right (do ask the O'Sheas for permission to pass through) leads on to the gentle slopes of Cummeennahillan (1,183 ft). Pause for views,

43 Glanmore Lake, with Tooth Mt behind

before continuing on the shoulder to Knocknaveacal (1,685 ft, hill of the teeth). The subtropical climate, here, has aided the development of the renowned Dereen House gardens, to the north. Its effects have also been felt in the thick undergrowth experienced on your ascent up to now. The remainder of your journey is, however, largely through barren bog and rock. You can ascend Tooth Mountain (1,945 ft) or take a direct line to Coomacloghane (1,969 ft), as the mood dictates.

Beneath you, to the south-east is the inner Cummeengeera valley, legendary hiding place of Sean an Rabach, a multiple murderer. Today only ruins remain of what was once a village, and the mood is one of undisturbed peace.

With views of Bantry Bay appearing on your right, descend now to the col and (avoiding if you wish Pt 1,956 ft) ascend to Pt 1,973 ft shown in the maps as Eskatarriff (Gully of the bull). You have for some time been following the Cork–Kerry border, but leave it now and continue east on the circuit. A steeper ascent leads to the highest point of the Horseshoe, Lackabane (1,984 ft, white flag stones). A gentler traverse to Curraghreague (1,970 ft) gives respite to admire the views of the Glanmore and the Lauragh area. Continue on to the shoulder (1,250-ft contour) before descending towards the stone circle of Shronebirrane. Alternatively, you can continue NNE to the woods at the north end of Glanmore Lake, through which a path gives access to the surfaced road.

This route is $8\frac{1}{2}$ miles in length, with 2,700 ft of ascent, and will take you about $4\frac{1}{2}$ hours, exclusive of halts.

Maps: 1″ Killarney District, $\frac{1}{2}$″ sheet 24.

From Kerry to Connemara

There is some fine scenery between the Dingle Peninsula and Connemara, but the hills, even by Irish standards, are small and really have no place in a book entitled *Irish Peaks*. However, any mountaineer who is not completely dedicated to high hills will find a visit to the Burren of Co. Clare well worth the time spent.

The Burren is a limestone karst set close to the sea, with a flora almost as unusual as the landscape which nurtures it. The moist, frost-free climate, combined with strong winds and the free drainage of the fissured limestone, provide a habitat where both arctic-alpine and Luso-Mediterranean plants can thrive. In May there is a particularly fine selection of species to be seen in flower – bloody cranesbill, mountain avens, stonecrops, rock rose, spring gentian and several orchids, while hidden in the grikes is the rare maidenhair fern. Please admire these plants *in situ* – DO NOT PICK THEM.

You can walk at will on the limestone pavements – Black Head and Slieve Carran, are a couple of suggestions. The Burren is also, of course, a fine area for caving – the Pollnagollum/Pollelva complex is big, even by world standards. A pleasant walk combining a variety of interests starts at the coast at the Ailladie (MR 090034) sea cliff (rock-climbing); goes inland across the limestone pavement (flowers); over Slieve Elva, whose shale summit caps the limestone (notice how the streams which flow on the boggy shale disappear as soon as they reach the limestone); and down east to the big Polnagollum pot-hole (not to be explored without proper equipment and knowledge).

A few miles away are the Cliffs of Moher, one of the most spectacular sights in the west of Ireland. They are 4 miles long and in places nearly 700 ft high. There is a car-park about half-way along, from which you can, in a few minutes, visit a natural viewing platform beneath O'Briens Tower.

Map: $\frac{1}{2}''$ sheet 14.

The Connemara Mountains

North and west from Galway the road runs as far as Maam Cross in a landscape of little hills, lakes, and bogland, with Lough Corrib forming the eastern boundary of Connemara on our right. Ahead, in complete contrast, rising directly from sea-level, is an apparently solid mass of mountains whose rocky quartzite slopes shine white in the sun. The westerly group, the Twelve Bens (everyone argues as to which amongst the fifteen or sixteen summits are the Twelve), is a square mass broken up by deep radial valleys, so that there are a number of fine horseshoe walks. The Bens are steep-sided hills with big drops between their conical summits and showing much bare quartzite. Apart from the two routes described, a south-north walk from Benlettery Hostel to Kylemore is recommended.

The Maumturks are similar in individual character, but are strung out in a long line of summits from Maam Cross to Leenane, providing one of the most challenging 'long walks' in Ireland.

Further north the Benchoona group offers less serious mountaineering, with fine views.

Bus services

From Galway these are fairly satisfactory. Buses run daily from Galway to Clifden, but they use a variety of routes and the chances are that the bus will be going via Leenane the day you want to go to Ballynahinch. However, with careful planning you can get yourself *into* the area by bus without much delay.

Car Access

The N59 from Galway to Clifden and on to Leenane and Westport provides excellent access to the area. Turn off at Recess on to the Lough Inagh road for Routes 23 and 24, while the start of Route 22 is actually on the N59. Route 25 can be reached by turning north off the N59 at Letterfrack, and Route 26 and the South Mayo mountains by following the L100 from Maam Cross direct to Leenane, through the impressive Maum Valley.

Accommodation

There are two youth hostels – Benlettery, near Ballynahinch, and
Killary. You would need to be a strong walker to get from one to
the other in a day! There are two Outdoor Pursuit Centres (Glen
Inagh and Little Killary) which might possible accommodate
walkers (ask in advance); and a bunkhouse at Leenane. As there
are quite a few 'B and Bs' you do not need to take a tent – though I
would suggest camping is the best form of accommodation in
Connemara. It is easy to buy food and drink, and camping places
are not too hard to find. Make sure first that your tent will keep out
the rain, second that your site is reasonably dry, and third that you
are not too near a stream that may rise overnight.

Maps

½″ sheet 10 covers the area – but most inadequately. Since distances
are short and slopes steep, there is hardly enough detail on the ½″
maps and this is perhaps one area where it is worth buying the old 1″
maps. Sheets 93 and 94 will see you through. The Maumturks are
on ½″ sheet 11 as well.

22 Glencoaghan Horseshoe (the Twelve Bens)

The Glencoaghan Horseshoe is deservedly one of the most popular
long walks in Connemara, taking in about 10 miles of walking,
5,000 ft of ascent, and six of the most impressive summits in the
Twelve Bens. The Benlettery Youth Hostel (MR 770484) is ideally
situated at the foot of the similarly named peak and the walker can
start the ascent on stepping out of the hostel.

A fairly easy slope will take you on to the main ridge which leads
to the summit of Benlettery (1,904 ft, *Beann Leitirigh*, mountain of
the wet hillside). At your back lies Ballynahinch Lake, cradled in
mature woodland against a backdrop of lake-studded bog and sea.

Bengower (2,184 ft, *Beann gabhair*, peak of the goat) is easily
reached along a broad ridge which curves north-eastwards and
steepens toward the summit.

A steep rocky descent followed by an equally tough ascent
carries you on to the summit of Benbreen (2,276 ft, *Beann
bruighin*, peak of the hostel) from where you can take in the

The Glencoaghan Horseshoe

44 Bencollaghduff (on left) from Benbreen. The route follows the ridge down to the head of the gully (Devil's Col), then climbs the steep face behind, towards Bencorr (extreme right)

glorious views of the surrounding peaks separated by the deep valleys of the Glencoaghan and Owenglin Rivers. The ridge curves away from Benbreen, first north-westwards over a minor summit and then north-eastwards towards a steep descent of rocks and heather to the broad, stony col below Bencollaghduff (2,290 ft, *Beann coileach dubh*, peak of the black grouse). The natural line along the Benbreen ridge takes you close to the edge of the precipitous cliffs which plunge almost sheer into the Owenglin valley, so tread carefully.

A broad, sweeping ridge rises to the summit of Bencollaghduff (plate 44). The south-eastward descent takes you across a wide expanse of smooth rock to the Devil's Col which overlooks some of the longest rock-climbs in Ireland at the head of Gleninagh. The climb to the rocky cone of Bencorr (2,336 ft, *Beann corr*, peak of the conical hill, plate 45) is steep but the summit is soon reached and the panorama of Lough Inagh and the Maumturk Mountains to

45 Derryclare (right) and Bencorr (centre), from Ballynahinch Lake

the east quickly takes the mind off aching limbs.

A 500-ft drop brings you face to face with the final steep, rocky ascent to the summit of Derryclare (2,200 ft, *Doirin clar*, wood of the plain, plate 45). From here you can descend to the Glencoaghan road via the easy ridge and Lop Rock, or take a steeper route down one of the gullies on the western face of the mountain, taking care to avoid any crags. The minor road will take you to the main Galway-Clifden road and so back to the hostel.

The Naismith time for this walk is almost 6 hours without halts, and because of the long descents and re-ascents between peaks it is quite demanding. You can shorten it by descending from the col between Benbreen and Bencollaghduff by the Glencoaghan valley, but the valley is very wet and boggy, and is not recommended.

Map: $\frac{1}{2}''$ sheet 10.

23 **Benbaun and Muckanaght** (the Twelve Bens)

Benbaun (2,395 ft, *Beann ban*, white mountain) is at the heart of
the Twelve Bens (plate 46) and its lofty summit commands the most
comprehensive views to be found in the region. To reach the peak,
car owners should take the track westwards at Barnaheskabaunia
on the Recess-Kylemore road, cross the new bridge which is marked

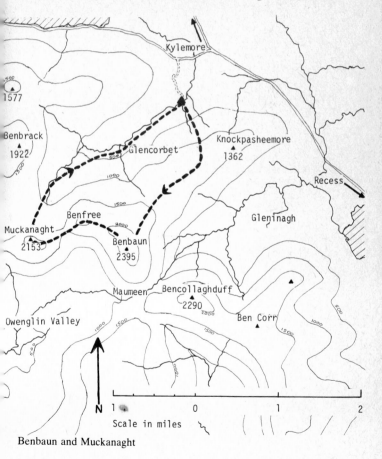

Benbaun and Muckanaght

46 The Twelve Bens, from Clifden. The deep gap in the middle of the range is Maumina, with Bencollaghduff on the right and Benbaun on the left

as a ford on the map, and park at an appropriate point near the Kylemore River.

Cross the bog to the foot of the Knockpasheemore-Benbaun ridge and pick a suitable line which will bring you to its peat-hagged crest. A somewhat tortuous walk leads to the foot of the scree-girt peak, which should be climbed with care. Benbaun (plate 47) is the highest summit in County Galway, and although not a high peak by Irish standards, you will find that it is a mountain well worth climbing.

From the summit take the gently curving ridge north-westwards to Benfree (2,000 ft) and descend to the col below Muckanaght (2,153 ft, *Muiceannach*, hill of the pigs). Here you will immediately notice a change in the terrain from the broken, quartzite slopes of Benbaun to the green, but equally steep, faces of Muckanaght. This is where the more hospitable schists, which are more typical of the lower ground, rise to more than 2,000 ft and allow plants to gain a foothold denied to them by the sterile quartzites of the surrounding peaks.

Take care on the ascent of Muckanaght, particularly in damp conditions when the ground can be very slippery. The summit is an excellent point from which to view the bays and islands to the north of Clifden. The northward descent is equally steep and should be made with caution. Once on the col below Benbrack, though, the going gets easier, although the ground at the head of the Kylemore River is often very wet. Follow the southern bank of the river, keeping to higher, drier ground when necessary, until you pick up the track which will return you to your starting point.

This walk is about 6 miles long, with 2,800 ft of ascent, and will take about 3 hours, excluding halts.

Map: $\frac{1}{2}''$ sheet 10.

47 Benbaun (left) and Bencollaghduff (right) from Muckanaght. The route follows the left skyline ridge from Benbaun

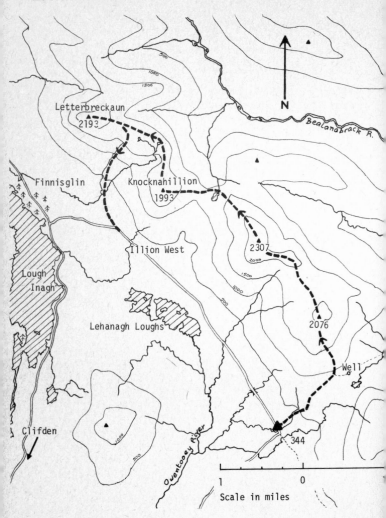

The Central Maumturks

24 **The Central Maumturks**

The Maumturk Mountains (plate 48) are often bypassed by walkers
visiting Connemara who are under the impression that the Twelve
Bens are the only range to climb in the area. How wrong they are!
The Maumturks offer equally good walking and scenery, and one
excellent route takes in the central section of the range from St
Patrick's Well (MR 904504) north-westwards to Letterbreckaun
(2,193 ft, *Leitir Brecan*, Brecan's wet hillside).

Approaching the region from Galway, turn right just before
Recess at Tullywee Bridge (MR 873472) and park near the
right-angle bend about 2 miles up the road. A track will take you up

48 The view from the Twelve Bens across Lough Inagh to the Central Maumturks, with
Letterbreckaun on left, Knocknahillion in the centre, and Pt 2307 on right

to St Patrick's Well at the col, from where the ascent to Pt 2,076 can begin. The ground is steep, heathery, and littered with boulders in places, but the first summit will soon be reached.

The ridge from Pt 2,076 to Pt 2,307 is easy going in fine weather and it commands an excellent view of the Inagh Valley and the Bens. But in mist it can be treacherous, and accurate navigation is essential if one is not to descend, inadvertently, into the Failmore Valley before reaching Pt 2,307. From Pt 2,307 the ridge continues north-westwards (plate 49) at an easy angle for about ¼-mile and then plunges steeply down to an unnamed rock-bound lough. The slope is scattered with small crags and loose rocks, and extreme care should be taken on the descent. Should you wish to retire from the ridge, this is the point from which to make the descent

49 Looking north from Pt 2307 to Knocknahillion (centre left) with Letterbreckaun (centre right) behind

south-westwards to Illion West, where you will pick up the road leading back to the start.

From the lough the ridge undulates somewhat and turns westward as it rises to the summit of Knocknahillion (1,993 ft, *Cnoc na huilline*, hill of the elbow). To the south there is a clear view of the lone hill of Lissoughter (1,314 ft, *Lios uachtar*, the upper fort), the site of a now derelict Connemara marble quarry.

From the summit of Knocknahillion the ridge continues its meanderings northwards to a small lough, and then veers westwards again to the summit to Letterbreckaun (2,193 ft). The summit cairn stands out prominently to the west of the natural route along the ridge, and accurate navigation is needed to locate it in misty conditions. There are fine views of the hills to the north and west and, particularly, of Benbaun standing sentinel at the head of Gleninagh.

Return by the same route to the first col and descend the steep rocky slope westwards until you meet the stream, which will lead you almost to the road before it turns north-westwards. Take the road through Illion West and Derryvoreada back to base.

This walk is some 11 miles long, with 3,600 ft of ascent, giving 5½ hours' walking time.

Map: $\frac{1}{2}''$ sheet 10 (or 11).

25 The Benchoona Horseshoe

Benchoona (1,919 ft, *Beann chuinne*, peak of the corner) offers a fairly short but enjoyable walk over quite steep ground. It is within easy walking distance of the Killary Youth Hostel at Rosroe (MR 770484) which is one of the most beautifully sited hostels in the country, at the mouth of Killary Harbour opposite the mass of Mweelrea. The walk offers superb views over the islands at the mouth of Killary, and of the three finest mountain groups in the area, Mweelrea to the north, the Maumturks to the east, and the Bens to the south.

The route starts from the coast road between Tully Cross and Killary at Mullaghglass (MR 726525, plate 50). Follow the track up beside the Keeraun river until it peters out, then turn east along a

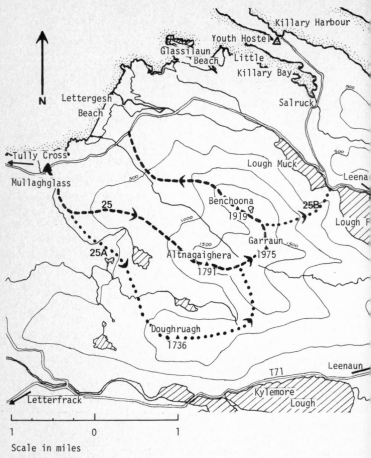

The Benchoona Horseshoe

gentle ridge, past the elbow joint of the river to the foot of the
jagged north-west ridge of Altnagaighera. Keeping to the right of
the crest, climb up grassy slopes, and then up one final steep slope

50 Benchoona from Mullaghglass: the walk starts opposite the nearest telegraph pole. The col between Garraun and Benchoona is on the extreme right

to the summit (1,791 ft). As you come over the crest the whole panorama of the Twelve Bens suddenly appears, with the chunky mass of Doughruagh (1,736 ft) close at hand.

From Altnagaighera walk east and south-east (good view of the rocky south-west face of Benchoona) along a broad boggy ridge to a rounded top, and then turn nearly north and climb up to Garraun (1,975 ft). There is a steep descent to a col, and then a gentle rise on to the summit plateau of Benchoona, a maze of outcrops and loughans amongst which it is very easy to lose direction. From the summit (1,919 ft) Mweelrea stands out to the north-east, and to the north-west the beaches and islands around the mouth of Killary are spread out like a map (plate 51).

There is a choice of descent routes. If you started from Killary Hostel, go back on your tracks a little way (Route 25B), and descend the steep ridge leading to the road between Loughs Fee

51   The summit view from Benchoona across Killary Harbour, Clare Island beyond

and Muck. Do not try to descend direct from the summit, the slope there steepens into dangerous wet and broken crags best left to the wild goats which can sometimes be seen on the ledges. The road back to the hostel, incidentally, passes a little Protestant church with a remarkable graveyard nearby. Here it was once customary for the mourners to smoke clay pipes after burials and then leave them at the grave. The graveyard is worth visiting to read the inscriptions on some of the headstones.

If you are returning to your car at Mullaghglass, descend the steep north-west ridge of Benchoona (keep a little right to avoid crags) to a gap. Turn left at the gap, and walk across the bog in a westerly direction until, beside the second stream which you meet, there is a track which leads you back to the road just above Lettergesh beach. A mile along the road to the west is your starting point.

The walk is 7 miles long, with 2,000 ft of ascent, and will take some $3\frac{1}{4}$ hours excluding halts. Using descent route 25B, it will take about $\frac{1}{2}$ an hour less.

A longer alternative (Route 25A) takes in Doughruagh, reached by continuing south-east across wet bogland from the first bend in the Keeraun river. Follow the chunky ridge from west to east (fine views of the Bens and the Maumturks), drop down to the col, and climb up again steeply on the north to rejoin the main route. Allow an extra hour.

Map: $\frac{1}{2}''$ sheet 10.

The Mountains of Mayo

Killary Harbour and the Maum Valley form the boundary between the quartzite mountains of Connemara and the sandstone of Murrisk and the Partry Mountains. The bare rocky slopes of the Bens are replaced by typical sandstone formations – boggy plateaux or rounded summits, both edged with dark, rocky, vegetated coums. We have picked three routes here, on Mweelrea (the highest mountain in Connaught), on Ben Gorm, and on the Devil's Mother (an outlier of Maumtrasna), but there is also enjoyable walking on the Sheeffry Hills or exploring the big coums of Maumtrasna.

Moving north, on either side of Clew Bay are the two isolated quartzite domes of Croagh Patrick and Nephin, and west of them the vast range of the Nephin Begs. From Mallarrany, at the south-west corner of the Nephin Begs, we cross the Corraun Peninsula, with its north-facing coums, to Achill Island. This is worth a visit for its beaches and sea-cliff scenery, as well as the two routes which we list.

Away north of the Nephin Begs are the sea-cliffs and hills of the North Mayo coast. They are not included in our list of 50 routes but take a look, if you have time, at Benwee Head or the curiously-named Glinsk.

Bus Services
Murrisk is badly served from Westport – you would be better off using Galway as a base – but one bus goes through Louisburgh to Killadoon, which would put you within striking distance of Mweelrea. North of Clew Bay there is a better service through Newport to Dooagh on Achill, giving reasonable access to Routes 31, 32 and 33. There is a service two days a week from Crossmolina to the foot of Nephin (route 30).

Car Access
The N59 from Westport towards Leenane feeds the South Mayo hills. Just before Aasleagh is the start of Route 26. Then at

Aasleagh the L100 branches off along the north shore of Killary, passing the starts, successively, of Routes 27, 28, and 28A, and then providing a return route through Louisburgh under Croagh Patrick to Westport.

The N59 in the other direction goes to Newport, past the start of Route 31, and across Achill Sound on to the island. The L141 goes out to Keem for Route 33, while the branch road north, the L141A, to Doogort serves Route 32.

Nephin (Route 30) can be approached from Castlebar (the L134/L140) or Crossmolina (the L140).

Accommodation
Killary Hostel is the wrong side of Killary Harbour for Mweelrea. Corraun Hostel is awkwardly placed for either Achill or the Nephin Begs; the only other hostel, Pollatomish, is too far north to be much use; but the new hostel at Treanlaur Lodge in the Nephin Beg range is well placed for Route 31.

Otherwise, it is hotels, guest-houses or 'B and Bs', and there is no shortage of these, though they may only be open in summer.

Maps
$\frac{1}{2}$" sheets 10 or 11 (South) and 6 (North) cover the area. There are no modern larger-scale maps.

26 The Devil's Mother
The Devil's Mother (plate 52) can be approached by several routes but the most direct is from the Leenane-Westport road starting to the north of Glenane (MR 912650). Follow a line up the steep slope to the left of the gully and climb steadily to the ridge where a short walk will bring you to the minor summit (1,983 ft). To the west are the dramatic corries of Ben Gorm and the Sheeffry Hills overlooking the headwaters of the Erriff (plate 53), a fine salmon river. The ridge-walk to the summit (2,131 ft) is easy and you will soon find yourself looking down on Lough Nafooey (*Loch na fuaithe*, lough of hate), a deep, dark, cold, lough famous for its large pike and also the home of the char, a small, trout-like fish which has

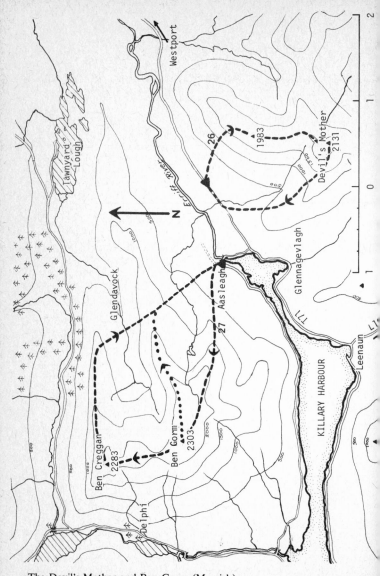

The Devil's Mother and Ben Gorm (Murrisk)

52 The Devil's Mother from across Killary Harbour. Pt 1983 is on the left, and the main summit on the right: the descent is by the lower ridge in the foreground

53 The Devil's Mother from the Erriff valley

survived from Ice Age times. The Finny River carries the waters of Lough Nafooey down to Lough Mask and directs your gaze eastwards to the narrow wooded isthmus which separates it from Lough Corrib.

To the north, the quartzite cone of Croagh Patrick rises majestically from the bogs of Murrisk. The white ribbon stretching to the summit bears witness to the efforts of many thousands of pilgrims who have tramped up the 'Reek' on the last Sunday in July each year. But the finest view from the Devil's Mother is of Killary Harbour sweeping quietly out to sea between the towering peaks of the Maumturks to the south and Ben Gorm and Mweelrea to the north.

Descend by the southern spur above the village of Glennagevlagh to the road, where a short walk will bring you back to your starting point. While you are in the neighbourhood, you should also visit the Aasleagh Falls, where you may sometimes see salmon leaping.

The walk is 4½ miles long with 2,200 ft of ascent, and will take about 2¾ hours, without halts.

If you want a longer walk, instead of descending, you can go east over Knocklaur and explore the huge Maumtrasna plateau. It is difficult walking, up and down over big peat hags, but there are compensations to be found in descending one of the big corries which fringe the plateau – Coum Gowlaun in the north west, Glenawough in the north, or the corries of the Owenbrin valley in the east.

Map: ½ sheets 10 or 11.

27 **Ben Gorm** (Murrisk) *See map on p 152*

This mountain immediately north of Killary Harbour must not be confused with Bengorm (Route 31) in the Nephin Beg range. Start this walk at the car-park (MR 893643) near Aasleagh Falls (*i as liath*, grey waterfall) at the head of Killary Harbour. Take the track to the north of the river for a short distance and move on to the hill towards the three Scots pine trees standing in such splendid isolation on the hillside. The slope steepens as you approach the ridge but the ascent is easy. The north face of the ridge is steep and

54 Ben Gorm (left) and Ben Creggan (right) from the north-east. The ascent follows the left skyline, and the Glenummera descent is by the ridge in front of Ben Gorm

rocky and care should be taken where the track passes close to the edge, particularly in windy conditions – which are the rule, rather than the exception. Ahead of you, the ice-picked corrie wall plunges 1,000 ft from the summit plateau of Ben Gorm (2,303 ft, *Beann gorm*, blue peak, plate 54), to the moraine-filled valley, and a stream tumbles down the rocky face to the dark lough below.

Behind you the River Erriff flows seawards at the foot of the Partry Mountains from its source in the foothills of Croagh Patrick. And below you, to the south, the sandbanks at the head of Killary Harbour are alternately submerged and exposed by the piston-like

action of the tides. As you approach the summit plateau the distant peaks of the Twelve Bens come into view beyond the northern slopes of the Maumturks, and on a clear day the Kylemore Pass extends the westward prospect to the sea.

The peat on the summit plateau is deeply dissected and can make navigation difficult, particularly in misty conditions when the summit cairn and the correct lines of descent are hard to find. In fact the summit cairn, which lies to the west of the plateau, is not the highest point.

From the summit it is possible to take several routes back to Aasleagh Falls. You can return by the route of ascent or by the central spur which offers a fine narrow ridge-walk with impressive views all round. Leave the ridge before reaching the end of the spur and return to base across the driest area of bog you can find. Alternatively, fitter walkers might like to continue northwards across the grassy col, past the remains of an old shepherd's hut, to Ben Creggan (2,283 ft, plate 55) and descend by the ridge overlooking Glenummera (*Gleann iomaire*, ridge glen, plate 54). Having now completed the easy part of the walk, your fitness and good humour will be tested by the final slog over the 2 miles of bog separating you from your starting point.

The short walk is 5 miles, with 2,300 ft of ascent, giving a walking time of 2¾ hours. Allow an extra 1¼ hours for the longer walk.

Map: ½″ sheets 10 or 11.

28 The Mweelrea Horseshoe

Mweelrea (2,688 ft, *An maol riabhach*, grey bald mountain) is the highest mountain in Connacht and it offers some of the best walking and scenery in the west of Ireland. However, walkers should also remember that an ascent of Mweelrea is a serious undertaking, particularly on short winter days, and they should be reasonably fit and well equipped when they set out for the summit.

One of the most popular routes starts at Delphi (MR 845666), just downstream of Doo Lough (plate 56). Cross the Bundorragha River

55 Ben Creggan from the west

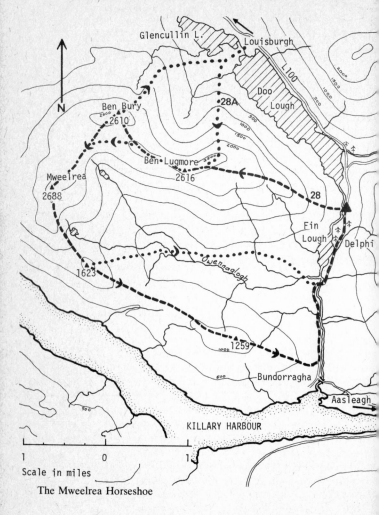

Glencullin L.

Louisburgh

L 100

Doo
Lough

Ben Bury
2610

28A

Ben Lugmore
2616

Mweelrea
2688

28

Fin
Lough

Delphi

1623

Owenaglogh

1259

Bundorragha

Aasleagh

KILLARY HARBOUR

1   0   1

Scale in miles

The Mweelrea Horseshoe

56 A view of Mweelrea (left, background) and Ben Lugmore (centre) from Delphi

57 The Mweelrea Horseshoe, from Benchoona. Route 28 follows the skyline to the summit on the left, and returns along the sunlit ridge in the foreground

58 Coum Dubh, on the north flank of Ben Bury

near a ruined building upstream of the lodge and move on to the
steep ground which will bring you to the main ridge early in the
climb. In mist, take care not to make the common mistake of
following the spur which runs south-eastwards from the minor
summit (2,616 ft, Ben Lugmore – name not on OS map).

The ridge is broad and undulating, and provides good walking
and excellent views to all points of the compass (plate 57). To your
right the edge of the ridge is dramatically marked by rugged cliffs
which plunge nearly 2,000 ft into Doo Lough, and to your left the
hillside falls away almost as steeply into the Owennaglogh Valley.

The ridge leads you to the second peak (2,610 ft: Ben Bury –
name not on OS map) but this can be bypassed to the south by
taking a direct line to the col below Mweelrea. A steep grassy slope
brings you to the summit of Mweelrea, which in itself is uninspiring.

However, the panorama from this lofty peak is breathtaking. To the west, the long grassy slopes sweep down to broad white sands fringed with Atlantic surf; to a rolling sea and rocky islands. To the east, the summit drops away sheer into the Owennaglogh valley. To the south, the mountains of Connemara stretch to the sea, and to the north, the rocky cone of Croagh Patrick reaches skywards as if attempting to make up that 178-ft lead held by its southern rival.

Descend by the steep southern ridge towards Pt 1,623 and, with Killary Harbour below you to the south, take the broad peat-hagged ridge over Pt 1,259 back to the road at Bundorragha. Alternatively from Pt 1,623 cross the valley and follow the dry ground to the north of the river back to Delphi.

This walk is 9½ miles long, with 4,000 ft of ascent. It will take a good 5½ hours without halts.

Another fine route up Mweelrea (Route 28A) starts from the road between Doo Lough and Glencullin Lake (MR 828696). Cross the river and climb the ridge leading to Ben Lugmore. This is steep going, and care is needed in selecting a route to avoid the crags on the ridge. The reward (plate 58) is fine views into the huge Coum Dubh (black coum). From the summit of Ben Lugmore follow the main route to the top of Mweelrea. Return to Ben Bury, and then descend the north ridge of this peak, thus completing the circuit of Coum Dubh. This ridge has an awkward step in it, that calls for the use of hands as well as feet. If this does not appeal to you, make a detour to the west, and then contour back; but all this side of the mountain is steep, and the route is not for beginners.

This alternative route is about 7½ miles long, with 3,700 ft of ascent, and will take 4½ hours, excluding halts.

Map: ½″ sheet 10.

29 Croagh Patrick

Croagh Patrick (2,510 ft, St Patrick's Rick, known also as The Reek) must have been climbed by more people than all the other mountains in Ireland put together. Every year on the last Sunday in July, thousands of people from all over Ireland climb the rough pilgrim path to the small chapel at the summit where they pray, hear

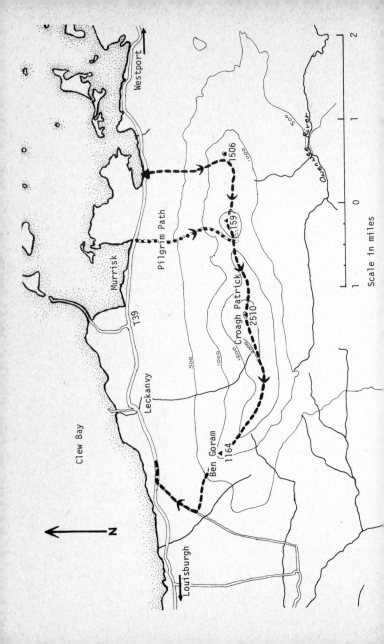

Clew Bay

Westport

Murrisk

Pilgrim Path

T39

Leckanvy

Croagh Patrick

Ben Goram
1164

1506

1157

2510

Owenwee River

500

1000

500

1000

1500

1000

Louisburgh

N

Scale in miles

2 1 0 1

59 The summit of Croagh Partick from the pilgrim path. Our route follows the skyline from left to right

Mass, and receive Communion, to honour St Patrick, Ireland's patron saint. The origin of this very ancient pilgrimage is not known for certain, but it is supposed to commemorate the banishment by St Patrick of all snakes from Ireland. Today, some of the pilgrims still walk barefoot over the sharp stones, but most wear stout shoes or boots nowadays – although after the walk is over the track is usually littered with such inappropriate footwear as high-heeled shoes and flimsy sandals. The pilgrimage is a spectacle worth seeing, but if you like solitude in the mountains The Reek is not the place to be on the last Sunday in July. Nor is the pilgrim path the best route

60 Croagh Patrick and the descent route, seen from Old Head

of ascent, unless your aim is to reach the summit in the shortest possible time. In fact, one of the most enjoyable routes runs along the whole ridge, with the summit of Croagh Patrick at the mid-point of the walk.

Starting in the east you should leave the road east of Murrisk (*Muirisc*, marshy seashore, MR 935823) and climb a steep spur to the minor summit of 1,597 ft. A short descent will bring you to the saddle where you join the pilgrim path (plate 59) which will bring you, slipping and sliding, to the haven of the chapel. This remains locked for all but the one day of the year. The view is superb. To the north, you look down on Clew Bay with its swarm of islands, each presenting a sheer face to the pounding Atlantic swell, while beyond the bay the bogs of Mayo rise to the lofty peaks of the Nephin Beg range. Guarding the entrance to Clew Bay is Clare Island, rising dramatically from the sea. Its history is as dramatic as its appearance, for it was the home of the great chieftainess Grainne O'Malley, whose exploits as a rebel and a sea-captain became a legend, and who is said to have dealt on equal terms with Queen Elizabeth I of England. To the south, the view is dominated by Mweelrea, the Sheeffry Hills, and the Maumtrasna tableland.

Continue westwards along the ridge (plate 60), then north-west towards Ben Goram (1,164 ft) and descend to the track which will return you to the coast road and your route back to base.

The walk is some 9 miles long, with 2,800 ft of ascent, and will take about 4½ hours, excluding halts, but including the road walk back to your starting point.

Map: ½″ sheet 10 or 11.

30 Nephin

Nephin (2,646 ft) is the second highest peak in Connacht and only 42 ft lower than Mweelrea. It stands in isolation to the east of the main mass of Mayo mountains and its almost perfect conical shape gives it a special aura. But although it is high and relatively steep, it does not provide the exciting walking one might expect and the summit can be reached easily in about an hour.

One of the most direct routes starts at the foot of the south-eastern slope (MR 123058). This point can be reached by a rough track running westwards from the Lahardaun–Levally road. Direct access to the mountain is now prevented by forestry plantations, so it is necessary to continue south-westwards along the track on foot, past a small white-washed building, to an inconspicuous gap in the plantation. The track passes through the plantation, across a stream and through a small farmyard on to the open rushy pastures at the foot of the hill. The rushes soon give way to heather, interspersed with patches of bog-moss, both of which make walking difficult. But, as the ground steepens the going gets easier and a fairly direct route to the left of the scree soon brings you to the main ridge. The route to the summit takes you along the

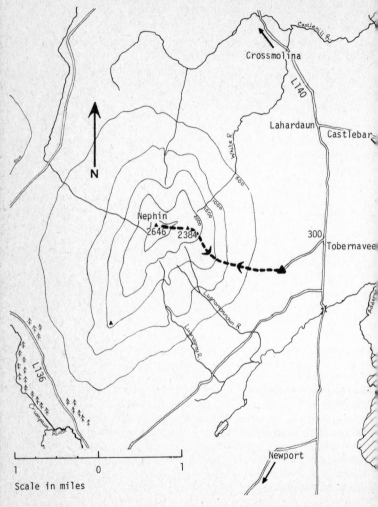

Scale in miles

Nephin

61 An aerial view of Nephin from the north-east. The ascent route is along the left skyline

rim of a deep north-facing corrie (plate 61) and care should be taken here in misty conditions.

In clear weather the views from the summit extend to Donegal in the north, Clare in the south, and to the heart of the Central Plain in the east. These are fine compensation for the rather uninteresting walk to the summit.

Descend by the same route, making sure that you move sufficiently far south along the ridge to avoid the crags and screes on the eastern slope.

This short walk of 4 miles and 2,500 ft of ascent should not take more than 2¾ hours.

Map: ½″ sheet 6.

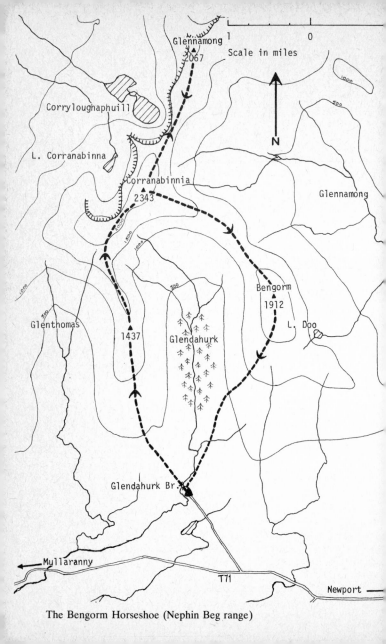

Glennamong
2067

Corryloughaphuill

L. Corranabinna

Corranabinnia
2343

Scale in miles
1

0

N

Glennamong

Bengorm
1912

L. Doo

Glenthomas

1437

Glendahurk

Glendahurk Br.

Mullaranny

T71

Newport

The Bengorm Horseshoe (Nephin Beg range)

62 The Nephin Beg range from Croagh Patrick

31 **The Bengorm Horseshoe** (Nephin Beg Range)

The start of this route can be reached by turning right up a track at
MR 923963 on the Newport–Mallaranny road. There is parking
space near a derelict house with a red tin roof. Take the track across
Glendahurk Bridge, through the turf banks, and move on to the
slopes of Pt 1,437. The walking is easy until you turn northwards on
to the final approach to the unnamed summit, Pt 2,343. The easy
slopes running down to Glenthomas give way to steep crags and the
sharp ridge offers an interesting challenge to the walker.

To the north and west, huge tracts of bog stretch to the sea, but to
the south the scenery is more varied, with the hills of south Mayo
providing a fine backdrop to the island-studded Clew Bay.

From Pt 2,343 (generally called Corranabinnia, from the nearby
lake) the Horseshoe continues south-eastwards, but the energetic
walker may like to continue northwards along the ridge to
Glennamong (2,067 ft). The ridge overlooks a series of crag-fringed
corrie lakes, an unexpected find amongst these rather rounded hills.

From the summit of Glennamong you look south-east across a valley full of young forest to Lough Feeagh; or north to Nephin Beg and the long ridge which leads far away to Bangor on the Belmullet road.

Returning to Pt 2,343, follow the Horseshoe south-east to a col at 1,200 ft, and then climb again to the summit of Bengorm. The valley enclosed by the Horseshoe has been transformed in recent decades from a brown, rolling bog to a sea of green conifers – a welcome change in this region. Descend the broad ridge, keeping to the south of the plantations and to the dry ground to the south of the river, which will lead you back to Glendahurk Bridge.

The route (including the diversion to Glennamong) is 10 miles, with 3,300 ft of ascent, and will probably take 5 hours, excluding halts.

This walk has only touched a portion of this wild and lonely range (plate 62). If you can arrange transport, drive up to Srahmore Lodge (MR 975043), set in a wonderful cirque of hills north of Lough Feeagh, and walk over Nephin Beg and the ridge to Bangor (MR 863232); or if you cannot spare time for this, at least drive along the forest road (marked as a footpath on the $\frac{1}{2}''$ map) north-east over the hills towards Crossmolina.

Map: $\frac{1}{2}''$ sheet 6.

32 Slievemore

The northernmost peak on Achill (*Achaill*, eagle) is Slievemore (2,204 ft, big mountain). It can be approached from Doogort (*Dubh gort*, black field) by the road running westwards along the shore to the quay (plate 63, MR 668389).

Climb the ridge to the left of the crags which drop sharply into the coum on your right. (These crags provide good rock-climbing, especially on the big buttress half-way up.) To your left the hill slopes more gently towards Keel Lough and Keel Strand (plate 64) but the instability of the ridge will be evident from the vertical fissures found on its rounded crest. The summit is quickly reached and your efforts are well repaid by the superb views – eastward to the Nephins, northwards to the Mullet and the Inishkea Islands, and southwards to the Mayo islands and Connemara.

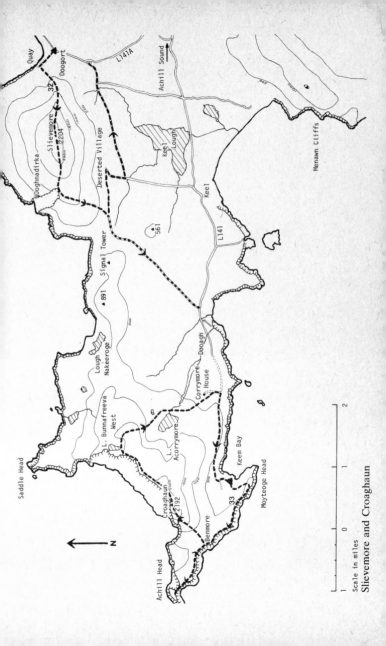

N

Quay

Doogort

L141A

Achill Sound

Slievemore
2204

Uoghnadirka

Deserted Village

Keel
Lough

Keel

561

L141

Signal Tower

▲891

Menawn Cliffs

Lough
Nakeeroge

Dooagh

Corrymore
House

L. Bunnafreeva
West

L. L.
Acorrymore

Saddle Head

Keem Bay

Croaghaun
2192

Benmore

Moyteoge Head

Achill Head

32

33

Scale in miles

1   0   1   2

Slievemore and Croaghaun

63 Slievemore, from Doogort: the route goes up the slope left of the crags

64 Slievemore from beyond Keel Strand. The deserted village lies below the left end of the hogsback of Slievemore

From the summit, descend westwards to the plateau, taking in the deep cleft in the mountainside to the north if you wish, and then turn south towards the deserted village at the foot of the hill (MR 640075). These deserted cottages, and the abandoned 'lazy beds' (fields where the thin soil has been scraped into a series of ridges to give enough depth for cultivation) are a very obvious sign of the depopulation which has afflicted the whole west of Ireland. A track leads westward from the village past a large quartz quarry to Dooagh on the south coast of the island, and this offers an alternative route to anyone not wishing to complete the circuit to Doogort. To return to base, though, take the track eastwards to the graveyard, turn right and then left, and follow the road back to Doogort.

65 Croaghaun, from Dooagh: the summit is centre background. On the right are the cliffs behind Lough Acorrymore

66 Keem Bay, Achill, with Moyteoge Head just in picture on the left, and Benmore on the right

This route is 7 miles, with 1,200 feet of ascent, and including the return to the road near Doogort, will take about 3½ hours.

Map: ½″ sheet 6.

33 **Croaghaun** *See map on p 171*

Croaghaun (2,192 ft, round hill, plate 65) offers the most interesting and spectacular walk on Achill, with steep slopes, narrow ridges, precipitous cliffs, and a spectacular corrie. Park near the secluded beach at Keem Bay (MR 560045, plate 66). Climb the steep grassy slope to the south towards the derelict Marconi signal tower on Moyteoge Head from where you will be able to appreciate the full splendour of the Menawn Cliffs to the east. Walk westwards and climb two steep steps to the high point of the ridge, Benmore. Take care not to venture too close to the steep gullies which fall directly to the sea nearly 1,000 ft below.

From Benmore descend to the boggy valley which will lead you on to the steep craggy slopes of Croaghaun. (An additional scramble along the knife-edge ridge leading to Achill Head should satisfy the adventurous walker before he tackles Croaghaun.) The summit cairn is situated at the edge of some of the most dramatic cliffs in the west of Ireland, which can only be properly appreciated when viewed from the sea. Continue along the cliff-top to Lough Bunnafreeva West and then turn south-east towards the rim of the spectacular, sharply ribbed corrie which cradles Lough Acorrymore (*Loch an coire mór*, lough of the big corrie). Follow the rim until you find a safe route by which to descend to the lough. Cross the mouth of the corrie towards the hotel and join the coast road which will take you back to Keem Bay.

The walk is 7 miles long with 2,500 ft of ascent, and will take about 3¾ hours, without halts.

Map: ½″ sheet 6.

The north-west

The North-west is a varied area, falling into no single geological category. In Sligo, the white limestone hills offer the rare luxury (in Ireland) of walks that are dry underfoot. Cuilcagh's bogs and vegetated cliffs are more in our usual style. The quartzite cliffs of Slieve League are unique, but as we head north and east we get back on to granite in the Bluestack and Derryveagh Mountains. The latter, in particular, are very rugged, with big cliffs, deep valleys, and rounded summit ridges dotted with small lakes, knolls, and crags. From Derryveagh we look north to the Errigal-Muckish group – steep, conical hills of very ancient metamorphic rock, perhaps the best walking area in Donegal.

Finally, there is the peninsula of Inishowen. There are better mountains to climb in Ireland than Slieve Snaght (Route 44), but it would be a pity not to visit this remote, wild peninsula with its fine cliff scenery and wide views. The whole Donegal coast, in fact, abounds in magnificent scenery, from the Fanad peninsula and Horn Head, past Aran Island, to the coast north of Glencolumbkille.

Bus Services
Twice-daily express bus services operate from Dublin. One route travels via Enniskillen to Donegal Town and the other to Letterkenny, via Monaghan and Lifford. This is also the quickest road route between Dublin and the north-west. Sligo is served by both bus and rail, and there is also an expressway interlink with other towns in the south. From Belfast, there are daily express buses to Londonderry, via Strabane. Both these centres, serving as 'gateways' to the Donegal Highlands, have connecting links to the Lough Swilly Omnibus Service which covers Inishowen and north Donegal, and to the CIE network serving south Donegal, Leitrim and Sligo.

Most of Inishowen's towns and villages are linked by a bus route, allowing the walker to explore the hill region of the far north

(Route 44). From Londonderry, twice-daily services (except Sundays) travel to Letterkenny and continue round the north coast through Dunfanaghy and Gortahork (Routes 42 and 43). From the latter, there is a bus through Gweedore to Dungloe, giving access to Route 41. A bus service south from Letterkenny goes to Gartan Lough with its forest park and the nearby Glenveagh National Park (Routes 39 and 40).

The south of Donegal, together with the Sligo/Leitrim area, is served by the CIE network. A route from Londonderry travels through east Donegal via Ballybofey and the Barnesmore Gap to Donegal Town and continues through Ballyshannon and Bundoran to Sligo. Two other routes serve west Donegal: one from Ballybofey travels to Portnoo on the scenic Dawros peninsula, via the Finn Valley (Route 38) and Glenties; the other follows the T72 westwards from Donegal Town, through Killybegs and Carrick, to terminate at Malinmore (Route 37).

A route from Sligo travels via Glencar (Route 35), Manorhamilton and Blacklion (Route 36) to Enniskillen.

Car Access

The three main centres, Sligo, Donegal Town, and Letterkenny, are all reached fairly easily from Dublin or Belfast.

From Sligo the N16 will take you to Castlegal (Route 35) and Cuilcagh (Route 36). Route 34 is just off the N15 north to Donegal. From Donegal Town the coast road N56 provides access first to Route 37 (Slieve League), then (by branching right near Gweebarra) through Doochary to the south-east side of the Derryveagh Mountains (Routes 39 and 40), and finally leads north to the Errigal-Muckish area (Routes 41, 42 and 43).

Heading north-east out of Donegal Town on the N15 leads you to the Bluestacks (Route 38) and eventually to Letterkenny, whence there is access west to the Glenveagh Mountains and Errigal.

Slieve Snaght Inishowen (Route 44) is served from Derry by the T73 (on the west) or the L79 (on the east).

Accommodation

There are a number of useful youth hostels. The Sligo area has none (the hostel at Glencar on sheet 7 is closed), but the YHANI hostel at Castle Archdale on Lower Lough Erne is not far from Cuilcagh. Carrick Youth hostel is close to Slieve League, and Ball Hill Hostel (Donegal Town) not impossibly far from the Bluestacks. Errigal Hostel is superbly situated between Errigal and the Poisoned Glen. Leaving aside our Routes, there is a string of hostels all down the beautiful Donegal coast – Bunnaton, Tra na Rossan, Aranmore (on the island) and Crohy Head.

Both the Sligo and Donegal coasts are tourist areas and are well served with hotel, guest-houses, 'B and Bs' and caravan parks.

Maps
Reading from north to south $\frac{1}{2}''$ sheets 1, 3 and 7 cover the area. NIOS 1" sheet 7 covers Cuilcagh – both sides of the Border.

34 Benwhiskin and Benbulbin
This walk, which makes the round of the summit plateau of the Benbulbin group, is noteworthy for the steep ascent on to, and descent from, the plateau, for the short, dry, limestone-based grass underfoot, and for its downward views on the steep scarps and ravines that edge the plateau.

Turn right off the N15 (T18) at Mullaghaneane crossroads about 4 miles north of Drumcliff and follow the road to the tiny village of Ballaghnatrillick (MR 739502). The Benwhiskin ridge (plate 67), which forms the western rampart of the Gleniff valley, overshadows the village like a petrified snow cornice. Park at the village, or drive along the road on the west side of Gleniff and park opposite the first cottage on the left. Access to Benwhiskin (1,702 ft) can be made by following the path to the cottage and then along the edge of coniferous plantation. The ascent is obvious, it is steep and yet not too difficult. As the top of the ridge is approached, care should be exercised on a windy day because very steep shaly limestone cliffs unexpectedly drop vertically for 500 ft on the western slope.

The panorama from this high point is excellent, with the crystalline rocks of the Donegal hills dominating the horizon to the north, while to the east Innishmurry Island looks like a giant submarine riding on the waves in Sligo Bay. Immediately below, a great patchwork quilt of green fields and dark hedgerows unfolds.

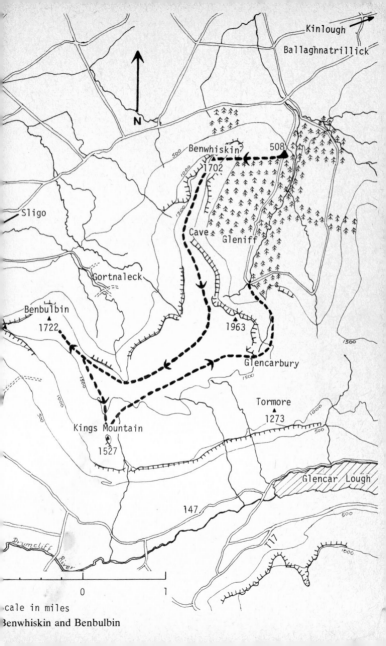

Kinlough

Ballaghnatrillick

N

Benwhiskin ▲ 508

500

1702

1000

Sligo

1500

Cave

Gleniff

Gortnaleck

Benbulbin ▲

1722

▲ 1963

1500

Glencarbury

1500

1500

Tormore

1273

Kings Mountain

1527

Glencar Lough

500

147

500

117

1000

Drumcliff River

0   1

cale in miles

Benwhiskin and Benbulbin

67 Benwhiskin, from the north-east

68 Kings Mt (left), with the slopes to Pt 1963 (right, background)

From here follow the broad back of the ridge for about ½ mile, as it runs south to meet the Poulhein cliffs. These reef limestone cliffs drop 1,000 ft to the valley floor and form a very fine cirque. Continue over a conical-shaped hummock and contour along the edge of the cliffs. Not far below the surface of this area of the mountain are three large caverns which are accessible from the valley below, through a big cave known as Diarmaid and Grainne's cave.

The route continues to a bowl-shaped depression which opens to the valley below through a large crack in the cliff walls. A descent into the valley from here can only be achieved by using ropes. The structure of this depression suggests that it is the remains of a collapsed cavern. The journey now turns south-west and continues over the Benbulbin plateau in the direction of Benbulbin Head. This part of the walk, which is approximately 1½ miles, circumvents the Gortnaleck valley and falls easily on to a wide saddle. The next leg of the journey is over a wide flat ridge which leads to the plateau of Benbulbin (1,722 ft). The plateau is edged by very steep and dangerous cliffs which are scarred by deep gullies. The descent of these gullies would be ill-advised as they end in very steep drops. The view is excellent but a more expansive one may be had by moving to the western spur of the plateau.

Backtracking along the ridge, the route turns south towards Kings Mountain (1,527 ft) with its unusual-shaped summit named Fionn Mac Cumhaill's Table (plate 68). The view from here takes in Glencar valley, Castlegal ridge, Sligo town, Knocknarea Hill and the Ox Mountains. Ascend from here in a north-east direction over undulating ground to the barytes mining works at Glencarbury. Barytes (barium sulphate) ore was extracted until recently by open-cast and tunnel mining. The descent from here is by the new miners' road which winds its way down into Gleniff valley and joins up with the Horseshoe circuit near the ruin of an old two-storey schoolhouse. From the ruin, a view can be had of Diarmaid and Grainne's cave high up in the western slopes. It is approximately 2 miles from here to Ballaghnatrillick.

The walk is 13 miles long, with approximately 2,200 ft of ascent, and will take about 5 hours exclusive of halts.

Map: ½″ sheet 7.

35 Castlegal Ridge

The Castlegal ridge outcrops on the southern slopes of Glencar valley and is very much in keeping with the character of the limestone hills of this area. It provides a wonderful view of Glencar and the limestone cliffs of Kings Mountain and Toremore (see Route 34). The starting point for this walk is approached by taking the N16 (Manorhamilton-Enniskillen) road from Sligo. On the ½″ to

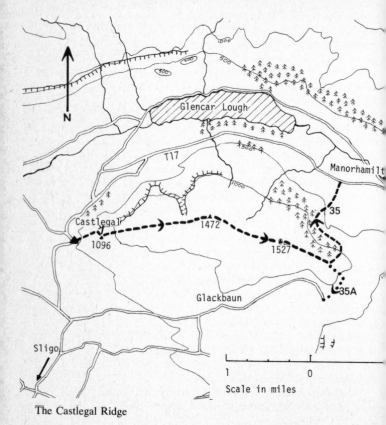

The Castlegal Ridge

69 Castlegal from the west. The track contouring the northern slopes is easily seen

1 mile map an S-bend is shown near the name 'Castlegal' (MR 725410). Its easternmost part designates the start of the hill route. On the ground a lay-by, an older and slightly higher section of this road, is located at this map reference. Walk along the old road for about 15 yards and cross an old wooden gate to gain access to the mountain slope. From here a narrow track leads up to an old ruin and joins a much wider one which turns south for a short distance before turning north across the slopes of Castlegal (plate 69). Ascend the steep ground by means of this north-bearing track until a stone wall is reached, and then turn south-east to reach the summit (1,096 ft). The view is enchanting, with a fine view of the Benbulbin plateau to the north, and it takes in Drumcliff Bay, Sligo town, Knocknarea Hill, the Ox Mountains and terminates with Slieve Killery and Da Ena on the southern shores of Lough Gill.

From the summit of Castlegal the route turns east over gently undulating ground (plate 70) for nearly 1½ miles, to high point 1,472 ft. This point is not very obvious on the ground. Changing to a south-easterly direction, the route descends into marshy valley and then climbs easily towards the grassy peak of Crockauns (1,527 ft)

70 Castlegal seen from the south, in snow. The route follows the skyline ridge from left to right

which is marked by a pile of stones. Here again the view of the surrounding countryside is very rewarding. Continue to the south-east for approximately 200 yards to a demolished stone wall, and follow its north-easterly run until it meets the corner of a well-built boundary wall. To the east, two conical peaks surmount each of the spurs which terminate the Castlegal ridge. The descent from here can be made by two routes and care will be needed because these spurs are bounded by very steep cliffs.

The usual descent route leads down into the Glencar valley via Lughnafangherry wood. With caution, follow the north-east wall towards the edge of very steep cliffs which drop into the forest below. After about 200 yards the wall ends suddenly, at the edge of a dangerous gully, and can be breached here through a wide gap.

Then follow a demolished wall which leads to the summit of the
north spur. Follow the wall from this summit until it meets a fence,
and then follow the fence down a small gully, on to grassy slopes
and along the edge of the plantation until a wide ride is reached.
The ride gradually changes to a cart track and then to a forest road.
This road winds its way down into the valley where it joins the
Glencar road near an old church. Follow the main road west, which
takes you high above Glencar Lough, back to your starting point
(there may be heavy traffic in summer).

Route 35A descends into Glackbaun. Starting from the corner of
the boundary wall, follow its southerly direction for about 400
yards, until it joins a boundary running south-east. The
south-eastern spur is bordered on its southern and eastern sides by
very steep cliffs. The view from the peak of the spur is worth taking
in, and the ascent from here should be by the north slope until a
fence is picked up again. Follow the boundary until it meets a
resurgent stream and contour south over the steep ground until a
tarred road is reached. This 4-mile road joins the N16 road about 1
mile south of the starting point.

Including the return road walk, the routes are each about 8½ miles
long, with 1,400 ft of ascent, and will take about 4 hours without
halts.

Map: ½″ sheet 7.

36 Cuilcagh

Cuilcagh (2,188 ft, *Cailceach*, chalky – perhaps from the white
appearance of some of the scarps) is the highest mountain between
Sligo and the Mournes and, with its scarps of Millstone Grit, and
interesting limestone scenery on the north side, is well worth
visiting. Be warned however that the going is rough and wet. The
route described is a traverse, which would be difficult without a
friendly car-driver to meet you at the end, but obviously ascent and
descent routes could be reversed.

From Blacklion (reached from Sligo on the N16 or Enniskillen on
the A4) follow the road on the south side of Lough Macnean
Lower. Take the right fork 2 miles from Blacklion and park at

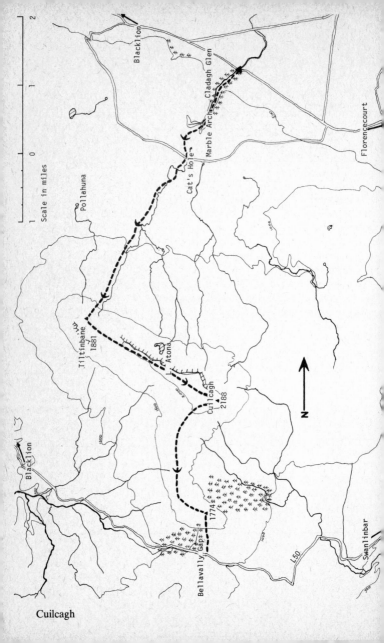

Cuilcagh

Cladagh Bridge (MR 128357). Walk up the Cladagh Glen through birch and ash woods; after a mile you will reach Marble Arch, a natural limestone bridge over the Sruh Croppa River.

The streams which flow down the Millstone Grit on the north side of Cuilcagh disappear underground when they reach the limestone, and most of them seem to reappear in the Cladagh Glen just above Marble Arch. The whole area is seamed with caves and potholes, several of which you will notice on your route. They are well documented in Gareth Jones' *The Caves of Fermanagh and Cavan*.

Climb south-west out of the woods above Marble Arch, and after a few hundred yards turn south, passing the Cat's Hole into which the Sruh Croppa River disappears. Notice the rich flora round this and other sink-holes. Next cross the Marlbank Loop road (the lazy could drive to this point, but it would be a pity to miss the Cladagh Glen) and continue up beside the Sruh Croppa (there is rock-climbing on Monastir crag, a little way east along the road).

Above the road, a 3-mile climb up rough, wet, heather slopes leads to Tiltinbane (1,881 ft) at the north-west end of the Cuilcagh ridge. Just to the west, incidentally, is the 'new' source of the Shannon; for the stream which rises north of Tiltibane and disappears into Pollahuna – 'Honeypot' (MR 089324) – has been proved by a dye test to re-emerge in Shannon Pot, the traditional source of the Shannon.

From Tiltinbane follow the scarped ridge south-east, with one foot in Northern Ireland, and the other in the Republic. There are fine views in both directions, over the Fermanagh Lakeland to the north and the mass of hills surrounding Lough Allen to the south. Beyond Cuilcagh Gap the ridge rises to the rock-strewn summit plateau of Cuilcagh, whence a new view opens to the south-east.

The descent is by the easy-angled ridge to the south, which drops gently to a saddle. This ridge is bounded on the east by a fine row of cliffs (plate 71). From the saddle there is a small rise over peat-hags to Pt 1,774, and then the route descends to the east of the wood to reach the road (L50) at Bellavally Gap (MR 122244).

The route as described is 9½ miles long, with 2,200 feet of ascent, and will take a good 4¼ hours without halts.

Note: the ascent route takes the same line as a section of the

71 Cuilcagh from the south-east

Ulster Way, and while it is not waymarked at the time of writing, it
probably will be marked within a few years. The descent route of
the Ulster Way from the summit will be towards Florencecourt.

Maps: ½″ sheet 7 and NI, 1″ sheet 7. NIOS 1:50,000 sheet 26,
Cuilcagh, is promised for 1983.

37 Slieve League

Slieve League (1,972 ft, *Sliabh liag*, mountain of the flagstones) is
the *pièce de résistance* of the Donegal coastline and ranks as one of
the finest marine cliffs in Europe. On the approach road (T72) west
of Killybegs (*Ceallabeaga*, little churches) there is little to indicate
that this lofty quartzite ridge has been gnawed away to its very core
on its south side by the ceaseless surge of the Atlantic.

The most popular and rewarding route to its summit traverses the
entire crest of the cliffs, and begins at the superb viewpoint of
Bunglass, (*Bunglas*, the end of the green). On arrival in Carrick,
turn left for Teelin. Ignore the signpost on the right, just before the
village, indicating Slieve League, as this track ends at the back of
the mountain; instead, turn right for Bunglass (2 miles) in Teelin
itself, and follow the adventurous metalled road which ascends the
lower slopes of the mountain. There is only one steep gradient.

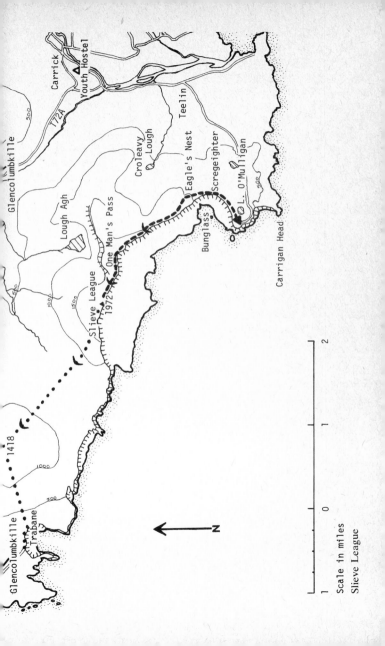

Glencolumbkille

Carrick

172A

Youth Hostel

500

Croleavy
Lough

Teelin

Lough Agh

Eagle's Nest

Slieve League

One Man's Pass

Scregeighter

1972

L. O'Mulligan

Bunglass

600

Carrigan Head

Glencolumbkille

1418

1000

500

Trabane

500

100

1500

500

N

Scale in miles

Slieve League

1	0	1	2

During its final stages it traverses the steep hillside high above the sea, with Carrigan Head and its old Signal Tower below on the left. Over the last rise, the road terminates at the small car-park beyond Lough O'Mulligan at the edge of Bunglass.

A few paces around the corner and the whole of Slieve League's immense façade bursts into view (plate 72). This spot, known as Awark More (the great view), fully justifies its name. The splendid cliffed face, extending for more than 2 miles, displays to perfection the quartz, schists, slates, and conglomerates of which the mountain is composed. These multi-coloured hues, combined with the staining of the mineral ores and the natural vegetation, give a fine spectrum of colours. At one's feet the twin sea-stacks known as the Giant's Desk and Chair are dwarfed by the Eagle's Nest – that section of the cliff which looks as if it has been cut by some cyclopean sword.

The broad summit is easily distinguished from Bunglass and lies west of the dipped arête on the ridge. It is this feature which is referred to on the 1″ map as the One Man's Pass. Seasoned ramblers can dismiss the rather exaggerated descriptions found in early guide-books of One Man's Pass being 'a narrow footway, high in the air, with awful abysses yawning on either side'. What is now recognized as a truer One Man's Pass is the short wedge of rock a little to the north of Crockrawer, which is illustrated in Vol. 2 of *Climbing in the British Isles* by H. C. Hart. West of the summit, cliffs of lesser stature leads to Rossarrell Point at the entrance to the horseshoe cove of Trabane (*Traig ban*, white strand) with its superb Silver Strand. Those who wish may walk the complete route from Bunglass to the Silver Strand, which includes the summit of Leahan (1,418 ft).

Leaving Bunglass, follow the track upwards through a mixture of rock and heather to Scregeighter (1,021 ft). Then follow the bend in the cliffs towards the Eagle's Nest (1,570 ft) Keep well away from its sheer drop in windy weather. A short descent follows, before contouring upwards and around the heather slopes towards the higher cliffs. A fairly well-defined track adheres mainly to the edge

72 The cliffs of Slieve League

73 On the ridge of Slieve League, looking down on Teelin

and is relatively straightforward. Soon the sharp rock rib of the One
Man's Pass appears ahead. It angles up for about 10 yards with a
precipitous drop on its seaward side. For anyone with a good head
for heights it should present no problem, but it can be bypassed on
the landward side. Continue along the crest with impressive views
eastwards over Teelin Harbour (plate 73) and the whole south coast
of Donegal. Beyond a large buttress the ridge broadens out. A little
to the north, and well worth a visit, are the remains of the oratory
and holy wells associated with St Assicus, who was appointed as a
goldsmith to St Patrick. He was reputed to have taken refuge on
Slieve League for seven years.

Regain the ridge and cross the peat-eroded top towards the arête
between the cliffs and Lough Agh, the corrie lake lying 1,500 ft

below the northern slopes. Its headwall gives shelter to an important colony of alpine plants which include the bear-berry, alpine meadow-rue, mountain aven, purple saxifrage and the green spleenwort. There is ample room on this One Man's Pass, and once across there is a level walk to the OS cairn on the summit (1,972 ft).

The panorama in clear weather is probably unsurpassed for variety on the west coast. Southwards, across the azure expanse of Donegal Bay one can observe the whole line of heights from the limestone hills behind Bundoran, past Benbulbin, to as far as Benwee Head and the Stacks of Broadhaven in outermost Mayo. On the southern horizon the hump of Nephin, lying a considerable distance inland, appears to rise from the coast. In exceptional conditions one can glimpse the conical peak of Croagh Patrick on the shores of Clew Bay 75 miles distant. Northwards, a veritable sea of ridges and valleys stretch away towards the familiar outlines of Errigal and Slieve Snaght. A short distance below the summit on the cliffed face, a series of residual pinnacles called the Chimneys make interesting photographic subjects. Walkers who do not wish to continue westwards to the road at the Silver Strand (MR 497800) should return to Bunglass by the outward route.

The route as far as Silver Strand is 6 miles long, with 2,000 ft of ascent, and you should allow 3 hours, excluding halts. The return route to Bunglass will take about the same time.

Map: $\frac{1}{2}''$ sheet 3.

38 The Croaghgorm or Bluestack Mountains

This group of hills forms the largest upland area in Donegal, and dominates the country to the north of Lough Eske (*Loch eisc*, lake of fish). From the lake the five 2,000-ft summits are hard to distinguish, because of their rounded profiles, and because they are masked by the foothills which conceal their true height. Perhaps this is why the nomenclature of the group is so uncertain. The $\frac{1}{2}''$ map names only Lavagh More, and the Vandeleur-Lynam list also differs slightly from the names we have used.

The terrain bears all the signs of having been heavily glaciated, particularly around Lough Belshade, where there are good

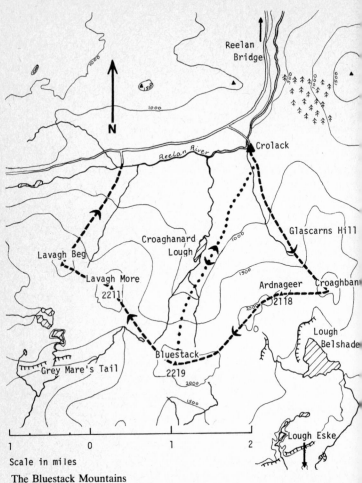

The Bluestack Mountains

74 The boiler-plate slabs near Lough Belshade

boiler-plate slabs for rock-climbing and scrambling (plate 74). The
lower slopes, however, of these hills are less attractive, being
generally very wet in winter.

The Bluestacks can be approached by a number of different
routes, including from the Effernagh River on the north side; or
from Lough Eske, via Edergole and the Eas Dunan waterfall on the
Corabber River to Lough Belshade (*Loch bél séad*, lake with the
jewel); or a more remote approach from the head of the Sruell
valley in the west, via the Grey Mare's Tail waterfall.

The first of these routes is our choice, because it traverses all the
five tops without retracing steps. It starts at the lonely farm
surrounded by conifers at Crolack, where the Effernagh River joins
the Reelan River. Access to the farm is reached by turning left past
the plantations, 3¾ miles west of Reelan Bridge on the back road
from Ballybofey to Glenties (MR 966963). A single track road is

then followed for 2¼ miles along the Reelan valley, until a rough track appears on the left leading to the farm over a narrow bridge. Vehicles can be driven across, and left near or at the farm (MR 963935).

Cross the field south of the farm and ascend the east bank of the Effernagh River alongside a series of small falls. Continue into the depression with Glascarns Hill on the left. Then climb to the top of Croaghbann (2,000-ft contour), with its summit lakelet (Lough Aduff). A short ascent to the west leads up the rocky outcrops to the top of Ardnageer (2,118 ft). Southwards, the vista includes the wild rock basin of Lough Belshade, with Lough Eske in the distance. Looking west, the grandeur of the broad main ridge is revealed, curving in an arc round to Lavagh Beg in the north-west.

Continue along the rocky crest towards Bluestack (2,219 ft), past a conspicuous white rock outcrop. About ¼-mile east of the summit, and a little below the ridge overlooking Croaghanard Lough, lie the shattered remains of an American aircraft which crashed early in the Second World War. Several small knolls are encountered before reaching the Bluestack cairn. The extensive panorama embraces much of Donegal's fretted coast, with the broad backs of Slieve League and Slieve Tooey dominant in the west. Northwards, over the Reelan valley and intervening ridges, rise the Glendowan and Derryveagh summits, with Errigal appearing to the left of Slieve Snaght.

On shorter winter days, a return to the farm can be made due north from Bluestack into the valley passing east of Croaghanard Lough, and hence to Crolack. Reaching Lavagh More (2,211 ft) requires a descent of some 600 ft to the north-west to reach the col at the head of the Sruell valley. The Grey Mare's Tail waterfall (plate 75) plunges down the south-west flank of Lavagh More. A climb then leads to the second highest point in the Bluestacks, with similar grand views. From here, an easy walk leads on to the flat-topped Lavagh Beg (2,000-ft contour), the terminal summit. The descent is best made to the north-east to reach the bridge over the Reelan River, west of the farm at the base of Lavagh More. Cross the bridge to join the road and follow it down the valley for about 1½ miles back to the starting point.

75 Approaching the Grey Mare's Tail, Bluestacks

The longer route is about 10 miles, including the road walk, with 3,000 ft of ascent, and will take about 5 hours exclusive of halts. The shorter route will take just over $3\frac{1}{2}$ hours.

Map: $\frac{1}{2}''$ sheet 3.

39 Slieve Snaght (Derryveagh)

The granite dome of Slieve Snaght (2,240 ft *Sliabh-snechta*, mountain of the snows, plate 76) is the principal summit of the Derryveagh range. As Donegal's second highest mountain, it rivals Errigal as one of the best viewpoints in the north-west. Its finest elevation is revealed from the road (L82) between Glenveagh and Gweedore, where it descends from the moors south-east of Errigal. Here the mountain lords it over Dunlewy, with its polished granite

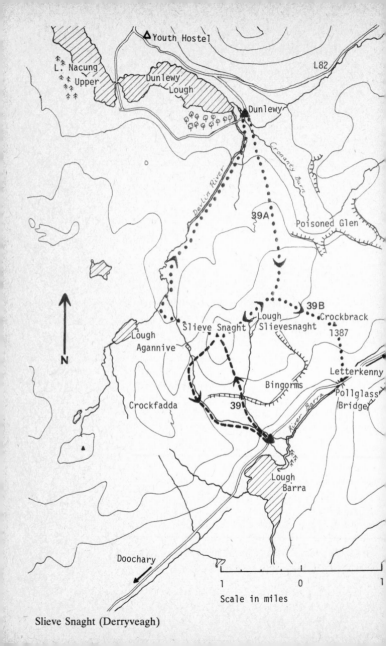

Slieve Snaght (Derryveagh)

76 Slieve Snaght (Derryveagh), from Errigal

slabs flashing like silver after sudden rain. It must not be confused
with the mountain of the same name in Inishowen (Route 44).

There are several ways of reaching its broad summit. The shorter
routes all start a little to the north-east of Lough Barra, which is
reached by an unclassified road, either from Doocharry in the
south-west, or from Letterkenny via Glendowan and over the
watershed above Glenveagh in the north-east. A much longer day's
walk (Route 39A) begins from the ruined Dunlewy Church and
follows the western side of the Poisoned Glen up on to the
intervening rocky tops, to reach Lough Slievesnaght east of the
main summit. A return can then be made down the north-west
flanks and along the banks of the wild Devlin River, which runs in a
gorge in its lower reaches before entering Dunlewy Lough.

The southern approach from Lough Barra is the more direct, with the added alternatives of rock- and gully-scrambling. It starts at the farm with its outbuildings (MR 936132). Immediately behind the farm lie the frowning granite buttresses and gullies of Bingorms, well known to rock-climbers as Lough Barra crag. It is possible to scramble to the top of the most obvious gully, although it is unpleasant except in dry weather. Those seeking a more gentle ascent should walk back down the road towards Lough Barra, and turn right at the bridge on to the bog. Walk up the river into the wide amphitheatre. After about ¾ mile a huge sweep of granite slabs can be seen on the right. These can be ascended with or without hands. It is not difficult to escape to either side if they become too steep (the left is better). Scramble over the rock wall and ascend steadily up the convex slope to reach the cairn on the summit (plate 77).

Northwards, beyond Dunlewy, runs the stately line of peaks from Errigal to Muckish, while turning to the west, you can see virtually the whole coast from the Bloody Foreland and the offshore islands to Tormore rock at the end of Slieve Tooey in the distant south-west. South-eastwards the elongated Moylenanav, (1,771 ft), a lone outlier of the Glendowan group, broods over the Gweebarra Valley. Its summit gives a dramatic view of this remarkable trough, which cannot be fully appreciated from Slieve Snaght.

The direct descent to the road now lies due south from the cairn, to reach the waterfall of the Scardangal Burn. Care should be exercised during the steep descent below the waterfall. Lower ground then leads around the western end of Bingorms to the road.

An alternative and longer descent (Route 39B) can be taken down the north-east slopes, to the northern shore of Lough Slievesnaght, and then following a broad ridge leading downhill to the left of it. Keep to the ridge, bearing right at the bottom, and observe ahead a deep gully into which an easy traverse can be made. The gully is split in three, the easy way out being to a little lough on the right (Lough Slievesnaght Beg). This is Rocky Cap mountain, which has an airy pinnacle after which the mountain is named. The next section lies to the south-east over bitty and broken ground to Crockbrack (1,387 ft) whose summit gives a good retrospective view of Slieve Snaght and Bingorms, with the steep northern flank

77 Looking north from the summit of Slieve Snaght (Derryveagh), to Errigal (left), Aghlas Mor and Beg (centre) and Muckish (right)

of Moylenanav across the valley. The descent continues south-west to reach the road at Pollglass Bridge about ½ mile north-east of the farm.

By the shortest route, the distance is 4 miles, with 2,000 ft of ascent, which will take about 2½ hours, excluding halts. The longer descent (Route 39B) to Lough Barra will take an extra ¾-hour. Route 39A from Dunlewy Church is about 6½ miles in length, with 2,000 ft of ascent, and will take about 3½ hours, exclusive of halts.

Map: ½″ sheet 1.

40 **Dooish**

Dooish (2,147 ft, *Dubh ais*, black hill) is the highest point on the long granite ridge running north east to Kingarrow (plate 78), parallel to the Calabber River. It is the principal summit within the recently established Glenveagh National Park. (You will find 'veagh' spelt variously 'veigh', 'beagh', or 'beigh' – even the OS map is not consistent. They all derive from the Irish *beith*, birch, and well illustrate the difficulties of transliteration. We have used 'veagh' throughout.) Until 1975, when it was purchased by the State, the

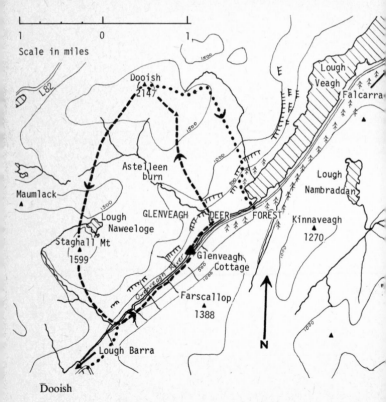

Dooish

78 A distant view of Dooish (background, right of centre) from the slopes of Slieve Snaght. Muckish and the Aghlas are on the left

Glenveagh Estate was a strictly preserved deer park. Several hundred red deer still roam here, living in natural conditions, enclosed within the 25,000 acres by a 26-mile fence. The estate lies around the impressive fault valley which has geological affinities with the Great Glen in Scotland.

Dooish can be approached from the L82 on the north-west, but it is a dull walk, and entails crossing the deer fence. The better, more dramatic approach, is via the Astelleen Burn at the south-west end of Lough Veagh. At the time of writing, prior permission to use the road to Glenveagh cottage (MR 993179) must be obtained from the Park Superintendent, as the Castle with its magnificent gardens, first laid out in 1890, are still in private ownership.

Passing through the estate entrance at the north-east end of the Lough, the road skirts the shore between gorse and rhododendrons.

79 Looking up Lough Veagh. The approach to our route from the Letterkenny–
Doocharry road is through the dip in the skyline

After about 1½ miles you reach the remarkable oasis surrounding
the Gothic-styled Glenveagh Castle in its unrivalled setting. John
George Adair, who built this fine edifice in 1870, had earlier gained
notoriety with the Glenveagh evictions, an unhappy episode in the
history of the north-west. Pass through the Castle gates, which are
flanked by stone eagles, with the pleasure gardens behind the
sheltering trees on the left. Continue through the Castle yard, and
beyond a gate the road becomes rougher. It continues to hug the
shore of the Lough, through a dense canopy of natural woodland.
Glenveagh is perhaps the gem of Donegal, and the Lough, amid its
wild setting of trees, crags, and forbidding hills, is far more Scottish
than Irish in character (plate 79).

  Two miles beyond the Castle, at the head of Lough Veagh, the
Astelleen Waterfall is seen tumbling down some 700 ft in three
stages, on the opposite side of the valley. This is the highest

waterfall in the north-west, a magnificent spectacle after heavy rain. Continue for another mile to Glenveagh cottage, where there is ample parking space and where the Owenveagh River can easily be crossed. An alternative, if permission cannot be got, is to park at the bend (MR 970157) on the Letterkenny–Doochary road (see Route 39) where it turns south-west towards Lough Barra, and to walk down the Owenveagh valley to join the main route. From the cottage, a short walk down the left bank leads to the base of the waterfall, to the right of which is an easy ascent. You should aim for the isolated boulder on the ridge, to the right of the waterfall (seen from the road). Scramble up to the bottom of the top section – there are a several inviting pools to splash in on a hot summer's day. Bear right, and, keeping to the vegetated area to avoid the rock, scramble up to the valley rim, to emerge near the boulder.

Head north, over a mixture of grass and flat rock, to the 1,750-ft contour, with the Astelleen Burn on the left, backed by Errigal. On gaining this top, the cairn on Dooish lies $\frac{1}{2}$-mile to the north-west. There is a slight descent over broken peaty ground, before the final climb to the summit. The best viewpoint however, is a little to the north, where far below you the desolate moor lies, threaded by the L82. The whole scene is backed by the distinctive chain of peaks from Errigal to Muckish. To the south-west, Maumlack (1,589 ft) masks the Poisoned Glen.

Those seeking a longer day's tramp can continue south-west around the head of the Astelleen Burn to the flat summit of Staghall (1,599 ft) beyond the high-level Lough Naweeloge with its island. Your descent then lies south into the upper part of Glenveagh. A shorter return route is via the conspicuously perched boulder $\frac{1}{2}$-mile to the south-east. On reaching this, descend into the depression and follow the Derrybeg Stream to the point where it plunges down through trees into Lough Veagh. Bear right from the top of the stream, angling down through tussocky grass towards the trees at the end of the lough. Cross the tawny beach, to reach the footbridge over the Owenveagh River, and walk up the road for $\frac{3}{4}$ mile to Glenveagh Cottage.

From Glenveagh Cottage the main route (including Staghall Mountain) is nearly 7 miles long, with 2,350 ft of ascent, and will take a good 3½ hours without halts. The shorter route will take ½–¾ hour less.

Map: ½″ sheet 1.

41 **Errigal**

Monarch of the north-west, the startling white peak of Errigal (2,466 ft, *Aireagál*, an oratory) comes into view on the L130, some 2 miles north of Crolly in the heart of the Rosses country (plate 80). Completely dominating this part of Donegal, with its air of sturdy isolation, it might at first sight be mistaken for some enormous shale bing. Its pyramidal form rising from the shores of Dunlewy Lough is an arresting sight, for it is the most symmetrically disposed of all Irish mountains. The precipitous screes of frost-shattered quartzite terminate in twin summits which are among the most exhilarating viewpoints in the north of Ireland, and which challenge the visiting hill-walker.

Two routes can be taken to the summit. The well known 'tourist route', which can be ascended in 1 to 1½ hours, lies up the easier south-east ridge, while the other, more demanding, approach via the north-west ridge offers scrambling on its upper reaches.

The 'tourist route' (Route 41) leads off the L82 where it climbs on to the moorland high above Dunlewy Lough. Ample parking is available at the large lay-by overlooking the roofless Dunlewy Church. The initial gradient is easier if you begin about ½ mile further east, but no further than the signposted track leading to Altan Farm (MR 952205). The most popular climb in the north-west still has no regular track on its lower slopes, so it is simply a matter of ascending over firm heather to the lowest part of the ridge connecting Errigal with its satellite, Mackoght (plate 81). However, marker posts have recently been erected from the road as far as the ridge, presaging a path perhaps. Bear left and climb through the loose screes, where a faint track winds upwards, opening up a widening panorama of the sterile grandeur enclosing Altan Lough (*Altán*, the little cliff) with Aghla More to the north. Higher up, past a small pinnacle, the track turns around a rock outcrop, and reaches the lowest part of the summit ridge at the Glover memorial cairn

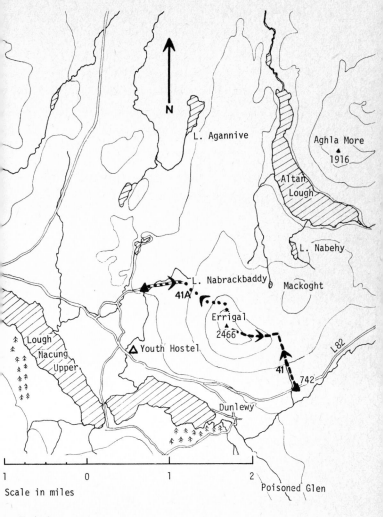

Errigal

80 Errigal from the south-west

81 Errigal (right) and Mackoght (left), from the north

beside a circular shelter. Joey Glover, founder in 1955 of the
North-West Mountaineering Club, had a unique knowledge of the
Donegal Highlands, and a pretty good acquaintanceship with the
rest of Ireland's hills. He was killed by the Provisional IRA in
November 1976.

The way to the summit now lies along an increasingly narrow
ridge. The allegedly higher of the twin summits was formerly
capped with an OS cairn; the second summit (which looks the same
height) is connected by a One Man's Pass of some 30 yards.

Errigal's summit, only a few feet across, must rank as the smallest
of the Irish peaks. It is a superlative viewpoint in clear weather,
embracing, it is claimed, all of Ulster's nine counties, with the Sligo
mountains on the southern horizon. Virtually the entire coast of
Donegal can be surveyed, from Malin Head to the ramparts of Glen
Head, with Tory Island off the north-west coast. Nearer at hand, the
bare rocky heights of the Derryveagh Mountains brood over the
savage crags of the Poisoned Glen. At one's feet can be seen the
causeway linking the twin lakes of Dunlewy and Nacung, whose
sparkling waters are backed by recent forest plantations, which
contrast with the natural woodland around Dunlewy House,
Northwards, a succession of conical peaks terminates at the broad
back of Muckish. Descent is either by the route of ascent, or, if you
prefer a traverse, by the route to the north-west described below.

The second, more arduous route (Route 41A) begins at the farm
beneath the north-west face. This is reached by bearing right at
McGeady's pub in Dunlewy (almost opposite the modern chapel),
and continuing uphill for $1\frac{1}{2}$ miles. Vehicles can be left at the road
fork, a short distance from the farm up a lane to the right. Once
through the farm and on to the heather slopes, there are a number
of possible ascents between the bare rock ribs and extensive screes
that characterize this side of the mountain, and with which the late
Joey Glover was so well acquainted. However, by bearing left, you
can gain the more obvious north-west ridge, thus avoiding the worst
of the screes.

Traverse across the screes towards the upper part of the ridge. If
you are keeping strictly to its crest, there are several places where
scrambling is necessary, but these can be bypassed on either side.

Higher up, if you look across to the adjacent rock rib, a keyhole can
be seen through the rock. Towards the top, the shattered ridge ends
at the smaller of the twin summits. If transport has previously been
arranged, it is a much pleasanter descent down the 'tourist route'.
Otherwise it is advisable to contour down the north face and around
the base of the north-west ridge, back to the starting point.

The routes are both about 2¼ miles long, with 1,800 ft of ascent,
and should take less than 2 hours, excluding halts.

Map: ½″ sheet 1.

42 Aghla More and Aghla Beg

This group of peaks is situated between Muckish Gap to the north
and Altan Lough to the south. They form a trio of elegant
mountains to the east of the L130 between Gweedore and
Falcarragh.

Aghla More (1,916 ft, *Eachla*, a stable), is connected by a level
ridge to the twin summits of Aghla Beg (1,860 ft) which are about ½
mile apart (plate 82). The approach to this group can be made by
the track leading to Altan Farm off the L82 east of Errigal, or by the
forestry road which runs parallel to their south-eastern flanks,
beginning from the road south of Muckish Gap. These two
approaches, however, both involve a longish walk. A route which
traverses all three tops and offers a much shorter approach, starts at
the bridge which crosses the Tullaghobegly River, just north of
Procklis Lough to the west of Aghla Beg (MR 936257). This is
reached by taking the road to Muckish Gap from Falcarragh (which
is on the N56), and turning right 1 mile outside the village. Drive
south for 3¼ miles, following the Tullaghobegly River to the bridge.
A little to the north of this bridge, a track leads east to a farm.
Follow this, and ascend over the moorland surrounding the western
slopes of Aghla Beg.

Steep but firm ground leads to the first and lower of the twin
summits (1,860 ft on the ½″ map). Follow along the ridge high above
Lough Aluirg, tucked under the north side of the peak, to reach the
higher, unmarked summit. North-eastwards, the intervening peak
of Crocknalaragagh (1,554 ft) masks the summit of Muckish Gap.

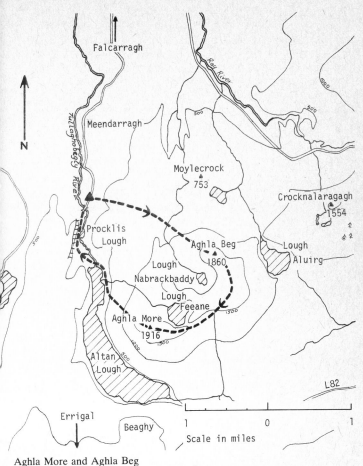

Aghla More and Aghla Beg

Now head south along the grassy ridge towards the cliffed shore of
Lough Feeane, the larger of the two loughs between the Aghlas. A
steep ascent leads past several eroded peat-hags to Aghla More,

82 Aghla More (left) with the two summits of Aghla Beg (centre) and Muckish behind, and with Altan Lough in the foreground

whose south side falls precipitously to Altan Lough. The summit is marked by a few stones. There is a superb vista over the Lough to Errigal's impressive north-east face, smothered in its mantle of angular screes, with the attendant peaks of Mackoght and Beaghy.

The descent from Aghla More is best made to the north-west down a mixture of rocks and heather to the shore of Altan Lough near its northern end. The stepping-stones at the river outlet can be used (unless covered by flood-water) to gain the road, across a few fields, at Procklis. Once on the road, it is a short walk back to the bridge.

This route is almost 6 miles long, with 1,950 ft of ascent, and will take about 3 hours exclusive of halts.

Map: $\frac{1}{2}$" sheet 1.

43 **Muckish**

Viewed across the broad waters of Sheep Haven in the vicinity of
Rosapenna, Muckish (2,197 ft, *Muc-ais*, pig's back) has an air of
slumbering graciousness compared with the austere grandeur of
Errigal and its neighbours (plate 83). It is the dominant landmark
on the north-west coast and rises abruptly from the moors as a
distinctive block mountain with a slightly tilted summit plateau. It
comes into view on the N56 going north out of Letterkenny, and
continues to command attention all along the coast as far as the
Bloody Foreland. Muckish's finest elevation is revealed on the road
between Falcarragh and Dunfanaghy, where it rises over an
entourage of lower ridges.

The two usual ascents begin at opposite ends. The first, and
easier, of these (Route 43) starts from the 810-ft summit of
Muckish Gap (MR 999268). Vehicles can be parked at the roadside
shrine, where an easy but steep ascent is taken up the south-east
spur. There are good views, especially to the west, through the
glacial breach of the Gap towards the coast. Once the stony wastes
of the plateau are reached, walk to the large central cairn, the top of
which might be mistaken for the summit. The real summit however,
can be seen across the boulder field to the north; it was once
indicated by a wooden cross, erected in 1950, of which now only the
stepped plinth remains. The immense panorama includes all the
intricacies of the north coast from Malin Head to the Bloody
Foreland, with the rugged promontory of Horn Head across the
New Lake. Southwards, the eye is led over the plateau to the
backbone of peaks and the sickle-shaped profile of Errigal. You can
return to Muckish Gap along the north-west edge of the plateau
(where you look down into the old workings of the former
sand-quarries) and then along the western edge to the south side
overlooking Muckish Gap.

The other route (Route 43A), which gives a steeper and more
direct ascent, is known as the Miners' Track route, and starts at the
base of the old sand-quarries on the north-west side of the
mountain. Fine quality silica sand, used in the manufacture of
optical glass, was extracted and shipped out of Sheep Haven until
the workings were abandoned after the last war. A metalled access

83 Muckish from the north-west. The Miners' Track goes up the re-entrant in the centre of the picture, hidden by the steep north face

84 The Miners' Track on Muckish

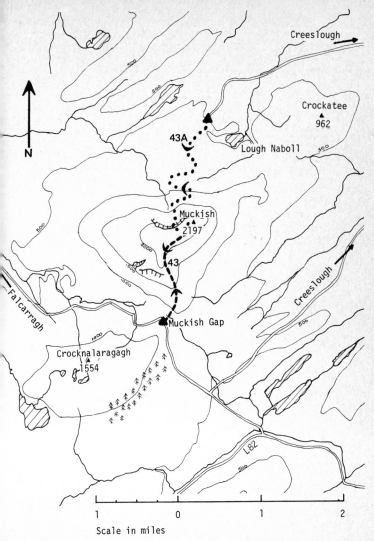

Muckish

road leads to the west of Lough Naboll, below the north front. This road leaves the N56 on the left about 1½ miles north-west of Creeslough (MR 050328), almost opposite the roofless chapel on the right. Drive along this road for 3½ miles, following the line of the abandoned Letterkenny & Burtonport Extension Railway, until the hard surface ends. Vehicles can be parked here. Walk up the rough road for about 1½ miles; it zigzags to the old concrete loading bays below a conspicuous cone of white sand. A prominent stone-filled gully on the left leads directly to the plateau. It is somewhat claustrophobic, and is best left to experienced scramblers. The so-called Miners' Track starts to the right of the sand cone. Higher up the mountain, its route can be picked out by a scant line of ruined safety posts. The initial route leads up past a pair of rusty tanks, and then follows up a spur, flanked by gullies on either side. Ascend the spur to reach the base of the rock face, and continue up the steep track (plate 84), which in places has roughly hewn steps. This section, which requires concentration, leads to the upper quarry. The eeriness of the desolate workings, surrounded by the silence of the encircling ochre-coloured cliffs, is enhanced by the occasional croak of the ravens which haunt these high places.

From the quarry, the faint track continues up the north side of this partly man-made amphitheatre, to reach the plateau. It is then a fairly level walk over the quartzite boulders to the summit. Unless you are descending to Muckish Gap, it is best to return by the same route, although an alternative descent, for those seeking a variation, can be taken down the northern nose. Then bear west across the slopes to the old loading bays.

Route 43A, up the Miners' Track and down to Muckish Gap, is 4 miles long, with an ascent of 1,700 ft, and will take 2¼ hours, excluding halts. Route 43, from and to Muckish Gap, will take perhaps 20 minutes less.

Map: ½″ sheet 1.

44 **Slieve Snaght** (Inishowen)

The most northerly of the Irish peaks, Slieve Snaght (2,019 ft, *Sliabh-snechta*, mountain of the snows), rises from swelling moorlands in the centre of Inishowen (*Inis Eoghain*, Owen's island) – that part of Donegal separated from the rest of the county by the deep indentations of Lough Swilly and Lough Foyle. The mountain is surrounded by a cluster of lesser hills which tend to disguise its true elevation. Its broad dome-like summit bears a passing resemblance to its namesake in the Derryveagh Mountains (Route 39) when viewed from across the western shores of Lough Swilly (plate 85). Slieve Snaght is heavily mantled in peat, so there is little of the bare rock that characterizes the majority of the Donegal summits. Its finest elevation can be seen from the vicinity of Carndonagh, where it assumes a more peaked appearance behind

85 Slieve Snaght (Inishowen) from the west

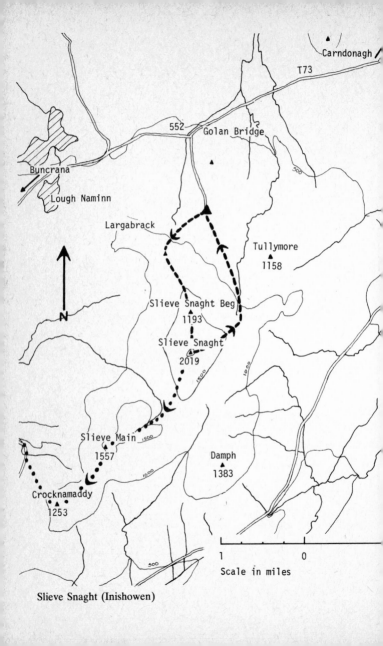

Carndonagh

T73

552

Golan Bridge

Buncrana

Lough Naminn

Largabrack

Tullymore
▲
1158

Slieve Snaght Beg
▲
1193

Slieve Snaght
▲
2019

N

Slieve Main
▲
1557

Damph
▲
1383

Crocknamaddy
▲
1253

1   0
Scale in miles

Slieve Snaght (Inishowen)

86 Nearing the summit of Slieve Snaght (Inishowen) with the Urris hills in the background

its northern outlier, Tullymore (1,158 ft).

The most convenient route to the summit is from the north, and lies off the road between Buncrana and Cardonagh. North of Buncrana, bear right off the T73 at Drumfree junction (MR 383390), and cross the moorland road to Golan Bridge (MR 424429). Turn right at the bridge, where a well-surfaced bog road can be walked or driven up for a mile. Vehicles can be turned and parked at the peat cuttings, beyond which the track deteriorates. From here, walk west over firm heather to gain the ridge descending from the satellite top of Slieve Snaght Beg, on the left. The two craggy outcrops, composed of metadolerite and seen to the west, are known locally as the King and Queen of the Mintiaghs. From Slieve Snaght Beg cairn, follow the bare slopes (plate 86) to reach the OS summit cairn on Slieve Snaght, surrounded by a stone shelter wall.

The wide panorama embraces almost the entire Inishowen peninsula, bounded to the west by the meandering Lough Swilly. All the main peaks of the Donegal highlands are arrayed beyond Mulroy Bay and dominated by Muckish and Errigal. Clear weather reveals also the whole north Irish coast, as far as Knocklayd in north Antrim, with Rathlin Island offshore. Far across the sea over Inishowen Head, one can glimpse the Hebridean islands of Islay, and Jura with its twin Paps.

Those who wish to make a longer day's tramp can continue down the south-west flanks, on over easy ground to Slieve Main (1,557 ft), and from there onwards to Crocknamaddy (1,253 ft). From the latter summit, a descent can be taken to the north-west to Fallask, where a road leads out to the T73. Previously arranged transport would be necessary here.

A shorter return to the starting point is made by descending to the small jumble of rocks on the north-east spur of Slieve Snaght. From here, head north down to lower ground between Slieve Snaght Beg and Tullymore, to join the end of the bog road leading to Golan Bridge.

The traverse from Golan Bridge to Fallask is a walk of 6 miles, with 1,850 ft of ascent, and should take 3 hours, exclusive of halts. Returning from the summit to Golan Bridge will take about 1 hr less.

Maps: $\frac{1}{2}''$ sheet 1.

The north

Moving east from Inishowen, across the Foyle and the Northern Ireland border, we come to the Sperrins (*Cnoc speirin*, pointed hills), perhaps the most unassuming of the Irish hill groups. Straddling the county boundary between Londonderry and Tyrone, they form an extensive area of boggy upland, partly grassy and partly heathery, running west from Lough Neagh to the Tyrone/Donegal border. Almost entirely composed of schist with a heavy covering of peat, and with little exposed rock except on the summit of Dart, the Sperrins invite comparison with the Wicklow Mountains in that their main attraction is to be found in the glens and wooded areas that lie around their base. The finest and longest of these glens is the scenic Glenelly Valley (Glen of the Stone Fortress), which forms the southern boundary of the main ridge. Long flanks characterize the main Sperrins, both on the north and south sides, and tend to mask the true elevation of the summits, five of which rise to over 2,000 ft. The main tops together with the Glenelly Valley, have now been designated as an Area of Outstanding Natural Beauty by the Northern Ireland Department of the Environment. The road traversing the south side of this valley gives the finest views of the main tops, which the granite outlier of Slieve Gallion (1,737 ft) south of Draperstown, provides a good scenic viewpoint of all the Sperrins.

Moving further east, we come to the lava flows and chalk cliffs of the Antrim hills and coast. There are no big hills here and we have listed no routes, but the reader who has toured Ireland with this book should certainly consider visiting the magnificent coastal scenery of the Giant's Causeway, Fair Head and Garron Point.

Bus Services
The Sperrins appear as a large blank in the criss-cross map of Ulsterbus services, but in fact on the north side, at least, the main ridge is not too badly served. A fairly frequent service from Londonderry through Claudy approaches the north side of the

range at Learmount and Feeny. On the west there are services from
Strabane to Ballynamallaght and Omagh to Plumbridge, both fairly
near the end of the Skyway (Route 45), while in the south-east the
Magherafelt-Draperstown service leaves you within striking
distance of the start of the Skyway. All these services are linked to
the express buses which cover Northern Ireland.

Car Access
The area is well served with roads. The A6 Belfast-Londonderry
road gives access to the north side of the area and there is a road
along the Glenelly Valley south of the main ridge. The start of the
Skyway is on the Feeny-Draperstown road, the end on the
Plumbridge–Dunnamanagh road, and the centre section of the ridge
is crossed by two minor roads.

Accommodation
Learmount Castle Youth Hostel is well placed for the Sperrins, and
Gortin (between Omagh and Plumbridge) is not impossibly distant.
If, as we suggest, you visit the Antrim coast, there is a series of
hostels from Whitepark Bay round to Ballygally near Larne.
Accommodation is plentiful here (though it may be full in the high
season). It is a little harder to find accommodation in the Sperrins.

Maps
NIOS 1″ sheet 2 for the Sperrins, 1:50,000 sheets 5 and 9 for the
North Antrim coast.

45 The Sperrin Ridge (Sperrin Skyway)
From the hill-walkers' point of view there is perhaps too much
uniformity in these smoothly outlined hills, partly owing to the
similarity in shape of their dozen or so summits (Dart Mountain
excepted) and partly owing to their rather monotonous peaty
surface. However this surface, though broken and bitty in many
places, is not inconveniently boggy, and in dry summer conditions
offers good going underfoot. There are other advantages: once up
on the ridge you can follow it from end to end without dropping
below the 1,000-ft contour, and in comparison with the Mournes,

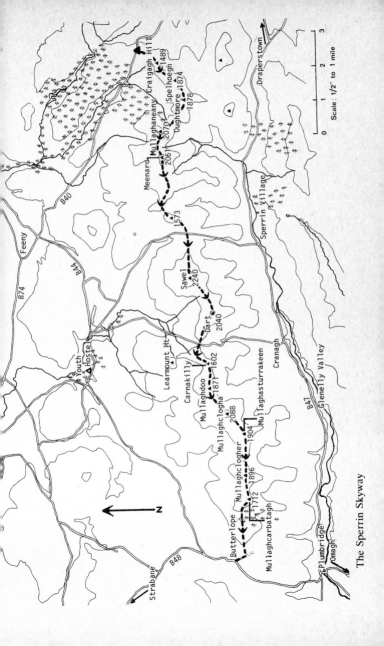

The Sperrin Skyway

Scale : 1/2" to 1 mile

0   1   2   3

N

Craigagh Hill 1489
Spelhoegh
Oughtmore 1874
1878
Mullaghaneany 2061
2010
Meenard

1573

Sawel 2240

Dart 2040

Learmount Mt.
Carnakilly
1602
Mullaghdoo 1871
Mullaghclogha 2088
Mullaghasturrakeen 1904
Mullaghclogher 1896
Butterlope 1712
Mullaghcarbatagh

Youth Hostel

Feeny

B40
B44
B74
B48

Strabane

Plumbridge
Omagh
B47
Glenelly Valley
Cranagh
Sperrin Village
Draperstown

87 A farm in the Glenelly valley, with the Sperrin ridge behind

for example, these hills are little frequented.

The Sperrins may be sampled by using one of the two roads which cross the range from the Glenelly Valley (plate 87) in the south to the village of Park in the north. The Sawel Pass road ascends gently from Sperrin village (Mount Hamilton), and the Dart Pass road, starting from Cranagh, reaches a height of 1,426 ft, making it one of the highest road passes in Ireland.

Starting from Dart Pass, a short ascent (about ¾-hour) south-east along the line of the county boundary fence leads to the summit of Dart Mountain (2,040 ft, *Darta*, mountain of the yearling heifers).

A walk of about 1½ miles to the north-east takes you to the OS cairn on the summit of Sawel (2,240 ft, *Sabhal*, a barn). This point can also be reached in about 1 hour by following the line of the same fence west from Sawel Pass.

In fine conditions, most of the north of Ireland is visible from Sawel, the view extending from Knocklayd in Co. Antrim to the Sligo mountains, and from the distant pyramid of Errigal in neighbouring Donegal to the serrated outline of the Mournes in Co. Down.

For those whose ambitions rise to a complete traverse of the range, Joey Glover, before his untimely death in 1976 (see page 209) worked out a most rewarding east-to-west route which runs for some 20 miles along all the summits. This he named the Sperrin Skyway and, though not yet an official walk, it may become one some day. In view of the rising number of entrants for the annual Mourne Wall Walk, it could provide a popular alternative. Opinions differ as to whether this is a desirable outcome. The Skyway has been traversed by some North-West MC members in 8 to 9 hours. Here are Joey Glover's suggestions, with some additional comments:

The route starts at the highest point on the Feeny–Draperstown road (MR 716997) and finishes at the Butterlope Glen, north of Plumbridge (MR 488954). It crosses all the five 2,000-ft summits, and conveniently divides itself into three sections: a) Starting point to Sawel Pass, b) Sawel Pass to Dart Pass, c) Dart Pass to Butterlope Glen. In addition to the two high-level roads across the ridge, there are a number of 'escape' roads on the south side (into Glenelly Valley) and one to the north.

The fence marking the county boundary between Counties Londonderry and Tyrone runs along a considerable part of the route, from Oughtmore (1,878 ft) to Carnakilly (1,602 ft). The exact starting point is at the end of a bog track running towards Craigagh Hill, and at least two vehicles could easily be parked here. The track gives out after about ¼ mile, and the way to the flat top of Craigagh Hill (1,489 ft) is fairly straightforward. A considerable drop (about 100 ft) down a steep grass slope next bars the way, but apart from one small dip, the rest of the route to Spelhoegh (1,874 ft) is simple and is marked by the new boundary fence on the right and the posts of the old fence on the left. The route and fence bear right towards Oughtmore (1,878 ft); there is a little bare bog on this section, but nothing troublesome.

At Oughtmore the route and fence bear right again; there is considerably more loss of ground between this and Mullaghaneany than the map indicates, with quite a marked nick at the lowest point. The fence indicates the easiest line, and should be followed to avoid entering a new forest plantation on the right. The summit of Mullaghaneany (2,070 ft) is marked by a few stones about 10 yards inside the fence. Between Mullaghaneany and Meenard (2,061 ft) there is quite a lot of bog, but nothing to impede you. West of Meenard there is another short stretch of bog culminating in a large and safe expanse of flat, exposed turf towards the 1,500-ft contour. From here, a straightforward descent leads to Sawel Pass.

The ascent of Sawel is a simple slog, and beyond it there is a further expanse of quite negotiable high-level bog. Dart is easily ascended; the route from this top to Dart Pass is broken in parts but is easy enough. From Dart Pass there is a fairly steady rise of about 1 in 10 for 3 miles over a nameless top, (1,616 ft), Carnakilly (1,602 ft) and Mullaghdoo (1,871 ft), to reach Mullaghclogha (2,088 ft). From the latter, head south-west for about a mile to gain Mullaghasturrakeen (1,904 ft). There then follows a considerable drop to the west, before ascending to Mullaghclogher (1,896 ft). From there on, you will have no problems and comparatively little bog to the final summit of Mullaghcarbatagh (1,712 ft), which has two cairns, with the larger one to the north. From the latter, head downhill to the west, following the fence for a while until it bears left. Keep straight on over firm ground to reach the road just above the hairpin bend at the summit of the Butterlope Glen.

The Skyway is 17½ miles in length, with 4,500 ft of ascent, giving a Naismith time of just over 8 hours.

Map: NI, 1″ sheet 2 (this will be replaced by 1:50,000 sheets 7, 8, 13, in 1983).

The Mourne Mountains

The Mourne Mountains are a compact group of granite hills offering many shortish walks with magnificent views. They are steep little hills, better provided with tracks than most Irish mountains, and, wonder of wonders, are mainly dry underfoot. They are 'civilized' and they are popular. The annual Mourne Wall Walk at the end of May attracts some 3,000 walkers, while the Reeks Walk and others attract only 100–200. There are likely to be many walkers on the hills, even on weekdays, since there are more than 20 Outdoor Pursuits centres around the Mournes, which collect all the walkers from Belfast. This popularity also means that farmers are less tolerant than in the west. Please do not walk across fields – access is really not too difficult anywhere if you follow lanes or tracks.

The Carlingford Hills are a completely separate range from the Mournes, but, situated as they are just across Carlingford Lough, it is convenient to include them in this section.

Bus Services
There are services two or three times daily (fewer on Sundays) around the perimeter of the Mournes. One service runs from Newcastle round the coast through Annalong to Kilkeel, meeting a service from Newry. Another service skirts the north side of the range (though at a greater distance) from Newcastle through Rathfriland and Hilltown to Newry. Both Newry and Newcastle are linked to Belfast by good bus services.

The Carlingford peninsula is served by about two buses daily from Dundalk to Newry and back, which might well save you some road-walking on Route 50. Dundalk is served by bus and rail from both Dublin and Belfast.

Car Access
There is an excellent road network around the Mournes, which are

split by the Hilltown-Kilkeel road (B27) past the Spelga Dam. The
Newcastle-Bryansford-Hilltown road (B180) gives access to Routes
47 and 49, while Route 48 is reached from the minor road which
runs across the mouth of the Silent and Annalong Valleys. Route 46
starts from the coast road (A2) which runs south and then west from
Newcastle, right round to Newry; and on the west the hills are
bounded by the minor road from Rostrevor to Kinnahalla, which
provides the return path for Route 49. The coast road, T62, from
Newry to Dundalk provides access to Route 50.

Accommodation
There are three youth hostels in the Mournes, unfortunately all on
the north side. Newcastle serves Route 46, Slievenaman serves
Route 47, and Kinnahalla serves Route 49. If you are a member of
a mountaineering club you will be able to use the Mountaineering
Club Huts, which are mostly on the south side of the mountains,
admirably placed for Route 48. Route 50 is well served by the
hostel at Omeath.

Newcastle is a seaside holiday town with lots of hotels and 'B and
Bs', and accommodation is quite widely available in the area.

Maps
The Mournes are admirably covered on the 1:25,000 Mourne
Country map. Slieve Foye is covered by the NI 1″, and by ½″ from
both Survey Offices.

46 **Slieve Donard** *See map on p 232*
Slieve Donard (2,796 ft) is the highest mountain in Northern
Ireland, and in the nine counties of Ulster for that matter. It is less
interesting than some of the other Mourne summits, but it
dominates the landscape from the north and its position beside
Newcastle (plate 88) suggests that we take it first.

Start from Bloody Bridge, about 3 miles south of Newcastle on
the coast road. The name comes from the massacre of 1641, when
Protestants from Newry and their minister were killed at the

88 Slieve Donard from the sea, with Newcastle in the foreground. The ascent route is up the left skyline ridge, its lower section hidden by Thomas's Mt in front

instigation of Sir Conn Magennis, whose family castle gave Newcastle its name.

Beside the bridge take a boreen which winds up past the Glenfoffany Climbing Club hut (now taken back by the farmer, and sold as a home). It continues past the old Bloody Bridge Youth Hostel, built by the devoted hands of YHANI members in the early '30s, but now closed, to the old quarries about 2 miles from the road. Granite quarries, mainly abandoned now, are very much a

part of the Mournes; in the past, grey Mourne granite setts paved Belfast streets, and granite provided the foundations for the Stormont Parliament Buildings. The track deteriorates as you climb on to the col between Chimney Rock and Slieve Donard, where you meet the Mourne Wall (plate 89). This stone wall was built by the Belfast Water Commissioners 60–70 years ago, to define the catchment area of their gathering grounds in the Silent and Annalong Valleys. It is a big solid dry-stone wall, 5 ft high in most places and 2 ft wide at the top. Many walkers prefer to use the top as a path rather than walk the muddy track beside it. For Donard, turn north (right) and climb steeply beside the wall to the summit. To the north-east of the summit is a ruined cairn (there used to be one on the summit also) associated with St Domangard (Donard), a fifth-century follower of St Patrick. The mountain was once known as 'Slibh Slanga' and the cairn was thought to be the burial place of Slainge, son of Partholan, who, according to the Annals of the Four Masters, died in Anno Mundi 2533 (that is, counting from the traditional creation of the Earth in 4004 BC). The view from Donard is very fine, embracing Galloway, the Lake District, the Isle of Man, and the Wicklow Hills.

Follow the wall west to the gap between Donard and Slieve Commedagh (admire the 'Castles of Commedagh', fantastic pinnacles of decaying granite on the south side of Commedagh) and turn north. On your left is the Pot of Pulgarve, and high on your right are the Eagle Rock crags, with many rock routes on them. Follow the track beside the Glen River into Donard Lodge woods, through which several tracks lead to Newcastle.

This route is about 10 miles long (including the road walk from Newcastle) with about 2,700 ft of ascent, and will take nearly 5 hours, excluding halts.

If you want more exercise, two side trips are possible. From the track between the quarry and the Mourne Wall you can walk up Chimney Rock Mountain (2,152 ft) and then return to the wall. Or, on the descent, instead of turning north down the Glen River, you could continue to the top of Slieve Commedagh (2,615 ft, mountain

89 The Mourne Wall

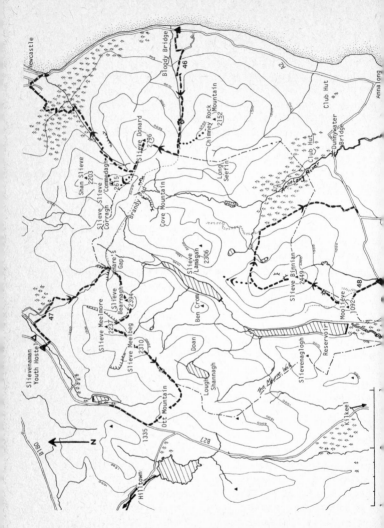

Slieve Donard, Slieve Bearnagh and Slieve Binnian

of watching) with new vistas opening up to the west and south. It is probably better to return by your upward route, as the slopes of Shan Slieve to the north and east are craggy.

Map: 1:25,000 Mourne Country.

47 **Slieve Bearnagh**

Slieve Bearnagh (2,394 ft, gapped mountain) is easily recognized from nearly any direction: its rocky tors with the gap between them are very obvious (plate 90).

90 Slieve Bearnagh from the north. Hare's Gap is left of centre; Bearnagh, with its distinctive gap between two tors, is on the skyline, right

The best place to start this walk is the Slievenaman Youth Hostel. From the hostel, cross the Shimna River by a footbridge, walk a few yards east along the road, and turn up the track beside the Trassey River. If you come by car, you can park near this track. On the right, as you walk up, you will see Spellack, an impressive crag with clean walls and vertical corners which has only recently yielded rock-climbs. Continue up to the Hare's Gap and, as you pass through the Wall, the whole central Mournes appear in front of you. The peaks of the centre fork of the trident – Cove, Lamagan, and Binnian – rise up ahead, with their steep flanks falling away to the hidden reservoirs of the Silent Valley. Contouring away to the east below the ridge of Commedagh is the Brandy Pad, an old track over which smugglers carried contraband alcohol inland from the small villages on the coast.

Turn your back on the Brandy Pad and follow the wall south-west towards Slieve Bearnagh. The slope is steep and rocky enough for the wall to be replaced by a wire fence, but by moving south you can avoid the awkward section. Bearnagh summit is topped by granite tors, on which there are some climbs; you can easily get to the top of the highest tor, from which there are spectacular views in all directions.

From Bearnagh walk steeply beside the wall down to the gap between it and Slieve Meelmore (plate 91). There is a rocky section near the bottom. Looking north-east back towards the Trassey valley, you can see the big mass of slabs on the northern slopes of Slieve Bearnagh. These slabs are a classic Mournes rock-climbing area.

Climb up beside the wall to the summit of Slieve Meelmore (2,237 ft, big bare mountain) and from there turn south-west along the ridge leading down to a gap and up to Slieve Meelbeg (2,310 ft, little bare mountain). These names seem to have become reversed, somehow, but in the past local people were probably more concerned with the bulk of the mountains than with their height, which they could not judge accurately anyhow.

It is possible to descend here, but this is not recommended as the slopes on the north-west are precipitous. It is much better to follow the ridge and the wall over Slieve Loughshannagh (mountain of the

91 Slieve Bearnagh from the slopes of Slieve Meelmore: the wall descending steeply from the summit tors to the gap can be clearly seen

lake of the foxes), round to the west on to Ott Mountain, and so down to the main road and a 3-mile walk back to the start.

Including the road walk, this route is about 9 miles long, with 3,100 ft of ascent, and will take some 4¾ hours, without halts.

Map: 1:25,000 Mourne Country.

48 **Slieve Binnian** *See map on p 232*

Slieve Binnian (2,449 ft, *Sliabh beinnin*, mountain of the little peak – presumably referring to the summit tor), viewed in profile from the west, looks like a prehistoric stegosaur, a huge reptile with armour-plate sticking out above its back (plate 92). Situated at the end of the middle fork of the Mourne trident, it is probably the best climb to choose in the Mournes if you can only manage one, both for the excellence of the view and for its distinctive character.

92 Slieve Binnian from the south-west, showing the 'armour-plated' ridge

Leave the Kilkeel-Hilltown road at the junction about 3½ miles north of Kilkeel, and drive east along a minor road past the entrance to the Silent Valley. Park about ¾ mile east of the entrance and follow the track going north (MR 319209). When you get on to open ground, either head up slightly left on to Moolieve, the first bump on the ridge, or, if you want a more exciting ascent, go slightly right towards the rocky summit of Little (or Wee) Binnian. The rocky face is split by a gully which gives an easy scramble to the summit. On either side of this gully are rock-climbs of some quality.

Having reached the top of Little Binnian, by one route or another, follow the wall on to Slieve Binnian itself. The slope gets steep as you approach the ridge, and you leave the wall to scramble up a slope to a gap between two of the tors. Although there are short rock routes on the sides of the tors, the ends are easy enough and you have the choice of avoiding them or scrambling over them. From the north end of the summit ridge, a slope descends gently, levels out, and then rises slightly to the North Tor, which is shaped like two squat watch-towers. There is a superb view (plate 93) from here north-west to Slieve Meelbeg, Meelmore, gapped Bearnagh and the Hare's Gap. The mass of Slieve Lamagan blocks the view north, but to the north-east Donard, a beautifully regular pyramid, dominates the Annalong Valley.

Continue north to the last tor, and then drop down east, passing Binnian Lough, until you come to a track above the forestry plantation which will lead you back to the road about $1\frac{1}{2}$ miles from your starting point.

This route is about 7 miles long with some 2,000 ft of ascent, and will take you nearly $3\frac{1}{2}$ hours, exclusive of halts.

There are several other possible walks (not marked on the map). For a short walk you can descend directly east from Binnian summit beside the Wall, but you miss the exhilarating walk along the ridge in exchange for saving $\frac{1}{2}$-hour. If you are fit you can continue north past Blue Lough, over Slieve Lamagan, Cove Mountain and Slieve Beg to the Brandy Pad. Then go right, below the Castles of Commedagh, climb up beside the Wall to the top of Slieve Donard, and return south along the Wall by Rocky Mountain and Long Seefin, to the road near Dunnywater Bridge. This will take you about $6\frac{1}{4}$ hours, excluding halts.

Of course, if you do not have to return to your starting point, you could descend from Donard to Newcastle or, instead of turning right along the Brandy Pad, you could turn left and go through the Hare's Gap and down to Slievenaman. Either of these fine walks through the middle of the Mournes will take a good 5 hours, excluding halts.

Map: 1:25,000 Mourne Country.

93 The view NNW from Binnian ridge. On the skyline are (left) Meelbeg, (centre) Meelmore, and (right) Bearnagh

49 Eagle Mountain

This is a good walk from Kinnahalla Youth Hostel (one of the few purpose-built hostels in Ireland) which explores a less-popular part of the Mournes.

From the hostel, cross the Bann and climb the slopes of Hen Mountain, with its several typical granite tors well known to rock-climbers. From the summit, head south-east for Cock Mountain (1,666 ft) and continue along the broad ridge to Pigeon Rock (1,753 ft). Below, on your left, is the Spelga Dam and the Deer's Meadow. This near-level bogland is named for the red deer which grazed there until, in the eighteenth century, the area became popular as summer grazing for cattle, which were driven up there from the neighbouring farms in the lowlands.

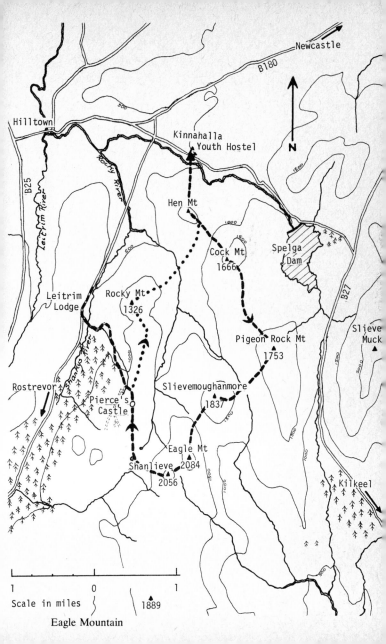

Newcastle

B180

Hilltown

Kinnahalla
▲ Youth Hostel

Rocky River

Hen Mt
▲

Cock Mt
▲
1666

Spelga
Dam

B25

Leitrim River

Leitrim
Lodge

Rocky Mt •
1326

Pigeon Rock Mt
▲
1753

Slieve
Muck
▲

B27

Rostrevor

Shanky River

Pierce's
Castle

Slievemoughanmore
▲
1837

Eagle Mt
╳ ▲
2084

Shanlieve
2056 ▲

Kilkeel

1

0

1

Scale in miles

▲ 1889

Eagle Mountain

94 Looking up White Water Valley to Pigeon Rock (right) and the ridge to Eagle Mt

From the grassy hogsback of Pigeon Rock, turn south-west towards Eagle Mountain (plate 94). The route climbs over Slievemoughanmore, drops to Windy Gap, and mounts a long slope to Eagle Mountain, at 2,084 ft the highest point of the Western Mournes. At your feet is a big crag which attracts both rock-climbers (for its long rock routes) and botanists (for its varied flora). Also, the peregrine has been known to nest there. Looking south-east, there is a fine view down the valley of the White Water to Kilkeel and the sea.

Continue south to Shanlieve (2,056 ft). The ridge stretches away, broad and level, towards Finlieve and Carlingford Lough, but our route goes west past the miniature Shan Lough, before turning north across Castle Bog to the granite tor of Pierce's Castle.

From here there is a choice of routes home. Go down the track which passes Castle bog and Altataggart, to wind down to the road near Leitrim Lodge, once a youth hostel. You now have a 2½-mile walk back to Kinnahalla. Alternatively, follow the ridge north to Rocky Mountain (1,326 ft), descend into the Rocky Water/Rowan Tree river valley, and either recross Hen Mountain or follow a track back to the road.

The route via Leitrim Lodge is 9¾ miles in length, with 3,500 ft of ascent, and will take a good 5 hours without halts. The alternative route is only marginally shorter.

Map: 1:25,000 Mourne Country.

50 **Slieve Foye** (Carlingford Mountain)

Across the narrow fiord of Carlingford Lough from the Mournes lies the long ridge of Slieve Foye and the rolling Cooley Hills. This was the scene of the *Táin Bó Cualgne* (the Cattle Raid of Cooley), the oldest Irish epic, dating from the time of Christ: it tells how Maebh, Queen of Connacht, made war on Concobar, King of Ulster, and on his henchman Cuchulainn, famous for his feats of strength and courage. The area is rich in prehistoric monuments.

The walk starts from the old town of Carlingford, which is dominated by a great Norman castle. Follow one of the streets going west and climb Slieve Foye from the south-east. From the summit, (1,935 ft) with its fine views of the Mournes (plate 95), walk north-west along the hummocky ridge to Pt 1,577 at its northern end. Then turn west across a boggy saddle to the Split Rock and Raven's Rock, outcrops of volcanic rock, and continue over Pt 1,330 (Foxes Rock) down to the road at Windy Gap. A megalithic chamber tomb here, the Long Woman's Grave, was destroyed in the making of the road.

From Windy Gap climb up on to Carnavaddy (1,568 ft, cairn of the hound), reputedly the burial place of Bran, the mastiff of Fionn MacCumhail. Fionn was the chief of the Fianna, a band of warriors who flourished in the time of the High King Cormac MacArt, about AD 300. Their exploits are the subject of many traditional stories. The ridge goes north-west of Clermont Carn (1,674 ft) and

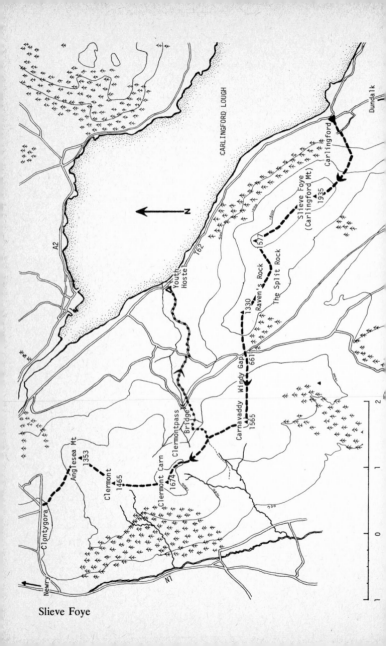

Slieve Foye

95 Looking back along the rocky ridge of Slieve Foye

Clermont (1,465 ft). If you have someone to meet you with a car, you can continue over Anglesea Mountain and down to Clontygora. There are two fine court-graves here, worth visiting. A mile or so further along the road is Flagstaff, a good rendezvous with your car, with magnificent views across Narrow Water and the Lough.

If you have to get back to your starting point, you would be better advised, after visiting Clermont Carn, to return to the Cadgers Road and follow it down to the road at Clermontpass bridge. This was the route used by herring-sellers bringing their fish inland from Omeath. Back roads will take you down to the youth hostel and the main road back to Carlingford.

This round trip, from Carlingford to Clermont Carn and back, is 14½ miles in length, with 3,400 feet of ascent, and you should allow 6¾ hours, excluding halts.

Map: NI, 1″ sheet 9 will about see you through, though the route spills over on to sheet 8, especially if you continue north from Clermont Carn. In 1983 NI 1:50,000 sheet 29 will be available.

Bibliography

General

COLEMAN, J. C., *The Mountains of Killarney*, Dundalk, 1948.

GILBERT, R. and WILSON, K. ed, *The Big Walks* (5 Irish walks included), London, 1980.

GILBERT, R. and WILSON, K. ed. *Classic Walks* (6 Irish Walks included), London 1982.

HART, H. C., *Climbing in the British Isles – Ireland* (re-issue), Dublin, 1974.

Irish Ramblers Club, *Dublin and Wicklow Mountains – Access Routes for the Hill Walker*, Dublin, 1976.

LYNAM, J., *The Twelve Bens – Hill Walks and Rock-Climbs*, Dublin, 1971.

MALONE, J. B., *Walking in Wicklow*, Dublin, 1964.

MULHOLLAND, H., *Guide to Eire's 3,000 ft. Mountains*, Birkenhead, 1981.

POCHIN MOULD, D. D. C., *The Mountains of Ireland* (re-issue), Dublin, 1976.

POUCHER, W. A., *Journey into Ireland*, London, 1953.

PRAEGER, R. LLOYD, *The Way that I Went* (re-issue), Dublin, 1969.

WALL, C. W., *Mountaineering in Ireland*, (this includes the Vandeleur-Lynam list of the 2,000 ft tops of Ireland), Dublin, 1976.

Irish Walk Guides:

South West, S. O SUILLEABHAIN, Dublin, 1978.

West, A. WHILDE, Dublin, 1978.

North West, P. SIMMS, G. FOLEY, Dublin, 1979.

North East, R. ROGERS, Dublin, 1980.

East, D. HERMAN, J. BOYDELL, M. CASEY, E. KENNEDY, Dublin, 1979.

South East, F. MARTINDALE, Dublin, 1979.

Background studies

BARTLETT, W. H., *The Scenery and Antiquities of Ireland*, London, c. 1840.

BRUNKER, J., *The Flora of Co. Wicklow*, Dundalk, 1950.

CHARLESWORTH, J. K., *The Geology of Ireland*, London, 1966.

COLEMAN, J. C., *The Caves of Ireland*, Tralee, 1965.

DONALDSON, F., *The Lusitanian Flora*, Dublin, 1977.

HORNE, R. R., *Geological Guide to the Dingle Peninsula*, Dublin, 1976.

HUTCHINSON, C., *Birds of Dublin and Wicklow*, Dublin, 1975.

JONES, G. L., *The Caves of Fermanagh and Cavan*, Enniskillen, 1974.

JOYCE, P. W., *Irish Names of Places* (3 volumes), (re-issue), London, 1973.

MACNEILL, M., *The Festival of Lughnasa*, Oxford, 1962.

MITCHELL, G. F., *The Irish Landscape*, London, 1961.

MORIARTY, C., *A Guide to Irish Birds*, Cork, 1967.

NEVILL, W. E., *Geology and Ireland*, Dublin, 1972.

O'ROURKE, F. J., *The Fauna of Ireland*, Cork, 1970.

PRAEGER, R. L., *The Botanist in Ireland*, Dublin, 1934.

ROHAN, P. K., *The Climate of Ireland*, Dublin, 1975.

TRATMAN, E.K. ed. *The Caves of North West Clare, Ireland*, Newton Abbot, n.d.

WEBB, D. A., *An Irish Flora*, Dundalk, 1977.

WHILDE, A., *Birds of Galway and Mayo*, Dublin, 1977.

WHITTOW, J. B., *Geology and Scenery in Ireland*, London, 1974.

Rock-climbing Guides

CONVERY, L. and LYNAM, J., *Bray Head and Minor Crags around Dublin*, Dublin, 1978.

FORSYTHE, J., *Mournes*, Dublin, 1980.

HIGGS, K., *Wicklow*, Dublin, 1982.

Irish Mountaineering Club, *Donegal*, Dublin, 1962.

LEONARD, J., *Malinbeg*, Dublin, 1979.

LYNAM, J., *Coum Gowlaun*, Dublin, 1969.

RYAN, T., *Burren Sea Cliff*, Dublin, 1978.

TORRANS, C. and SHERIDAN, C., *Antrim Coast*, Dublin, 1981.

YOUNG, S., *Dalkey*, Dublin, 1980.

Index